@**Copyright 2020by** Christy Markle- **All rights reserved.**

This document is geared towards providing exact and reliable information in regards to the topic and issue covered. The publication is sold with the idea that the publisher is not required to render accounting, officially permitted, or otherwise, qualified services. If advice is necessary, legal or professional, a practiced individual in the profession should be ordered.

Under no circumstance will any legal responsibility or blame be held against the publisher for any reparation, damages, or monetary loss due to the information herein, either directly or indirectly.

Legal Notice: The book is copyright protected. This is only for personal use. You cannot amend, distribute, sell, use, quote or paraphrase any part or the content within this book without the consent of the author.

Disclaimer Notice: Please note the information contained within this document is for educational and entertainment purposes only. Every attempt has been made to provide accurate, up to date and reliable complete information. No warranties of any kind are expressed or implied. Readers acknowledge that the author is not engaging in the rendering of legal, financial, medical or professional advice. The content of this book has been derived from various sources. Please consult a licensed professional before attempting any techniques outlined in this book.

CONTENTS

Introduction 6
Cooking with Instant Pot Air Fryer Crisp 8
FAQ: Instant Pot Air Fryer Crisp & Food 10
    How many appliances does the Duo Crisp+ Air Fryer replace? 10
    Why do I need to do the Initial Test Run? 10
    Can I use third party accessories with my Instant Pot? 10
    How much food and liquid should be in the inner pot when cooking? 11
    Are the parts from different models of Instant Pot interchangeable? 12
    What is the inner pot made of? 12
    Can I adjust my settings after cooking has started? 13
    How do I know if the pressure cooking process has started? 13
    How do I know when it's safe to open the lid after pressure cooking? 13
    Are there any foods I can't put into the Instant Pot? 14
Breakfast and Brunch 15
    Bacon and Croissant 15
    Air-Fried French Toast Sticks 16
    Ranchero Wraps 17
    Garlic Bread 18
    Shrimp and Rice Breakfast Frittata 18
    Omelette in Bread Cups 19
    Mixed Berry Muffins 20
    Dutch Pancake 21
    Spinach and Cheese Omelette 21
    Baked Eggs 22
    Breakfast Soufflé 22
    Cinnamon Toast 23
    Turkey Burrito 23
Vegetables Recipes 24
    Cauliflower Bites 24
    Buttered Carrot-Zucchini with Mayo 25
    Sage-Butter Spaghetti Squash 26
    Cheddar, Squash, And Zucchini Casserole 27
    Zucchini Parmesan Chips 28
    Jalapeño Cheese Balls 29

- Crispy Roasted Broccoli 30
- Creamy And Cheese Broccoli Bake 31
- Coconut Battered Cauliflower Bites 32
- Crispy Jalapeno Coins 33
- Buffalo Cauliflower 34
- Crisped Baked Cheese Stuffed Chile Pepper 35
- Jicama Fries 36
- Jumbo Stuffed Mushrooms 37
- Air Fryer Brussels Sprouts 38
- Spaghetti Squash Tots 39
- Crispy And Healthy Avocado Fingers 40
- Onion Rings 41
- Cinnamon Butternut Squash Fries 42
- Roasted Asparagus 42
- Crispy Broccoli 43
- Acorn Squash 43

Fish and Seafood 44

- Air Fryer Salmon 44
- Fish Finger Sandwich 45
- Tuna Patties 46
- Grilled Cod with Sauce 46
- Ranch Air Fryer Fish Fillets 47
- Tasty Cod 48
- Delicious Catfish 49
- Tabasco Shrimp 49
- Buttered Shrimp Skewers 50
- Asian Salmon 50
- Air Fried Salmon 51
- Lemony Saba Fish 51
- Asian Halibut 52
- Shrimp and Crab Mix 53
- Seafood Casserole 54
- Crispy Cheesy Fish Fingers 55
- Panko-Crusted Tilapia 56
- Potato Crusted Salmon 57
- Salmon Croquettes 58
- Snapper Scampi 59

Poultry Recipes 60
    Thanksgiving Turkey 60
    Turkey Burgers 61
    Honey Duck Breasts 61
    Chinese Duck Legs 62
    Duck Breasts with Endives 63
    Creamy Coconut Chicken 63
    Chinese Chicken Wings 64
    Herbed Chicken 64
    Chicken Parmesan 65
    Mexican Chicken 66
    Italian Chicken 67
    Chicken Salad 68
    Buffalo Chicken Tenders 69
    Teriyaki Wings 69
    Lemony Drumsticks 70
    Crispy Southern Fried Chicken 71
    Chicken Roast with Pineapple Salsa 72

Beef, Lamb and Pork 73
    Lamb with Veggies 73
    Creamy Lamb 74
    Lamb Shanks 75
    Lamb with Potatoes 76
    Classic Mini Meatloaf 77
    Chorizo and Beef Burger 78
    Stuffed Peppers 79
    Italian Stuffed Bell Peppers 80
    Bacon Casserole 81
    Spicy Lamb Sirloin Steak 82
    Herb Rack of Lamb 82
    Pulled Pork 83
    Baby Back Ribs 83
    Juicy Pork Chops 84
    Reverse Seared Ribeye 85
    Beef and Broccoli Stir-Fry 86
    BBQ Meatballs 87
    Pork Salad 88

Snacksand Appetizer **89**
    Prosciutto-Parmesan Asparagus.. 89
    Bacon-Wrapped Jalapeno Poppers 90
    Garlic Parmesan Chicken Wings 90
    Buffalo Chicken Dip... 91
    Cheese Bread 91
    Cheeseburger Dip 92
    Pork Rind Tortillas 93
    Mozzarella Sticks 93
    Bacon-Wrapped Onion Rings 94
    Sweet Pepper Poppers 94
    Spicy Spinach Artichoke Dip 95
    Potato Wedges 95
    Mushroom Dish 96
    Sweet Potato Fries 97
    Corn with Lime and Cheese 97

Desserts **98**
    Mug Cake 98
    Pound Cake 99
    Chocolate Mayo Cake.. 99
    Raspberry Danish Bites 100
    Peanut Butter Cookies 100
    Cinnamon Cream Puffs... 101
    Molten Lava Cakes.. 102
    Chocolate Cake II.. 103
    Cheesecake Bites 104
    Brownies 104

INTRODUCTION

The Instant Pot Duo Crisp + Air Fryer is the best of all possible worlds. With 11-in-1 functionality it does everything a regular Instant Pot does, but swap out the pressure cooker lid for the innovative air fryer lid, and you've got a whole new set of cooking techniques available — all fast, easy and at the touch of a button.

Now you have every cooking method available at your fingertips. The pressure cooker lid offers 6 wet cooking functions: use it to quickly pressure cook, sauté, steam, slow cook, sous vide and warm. The Air Fryer lid offers 5 crisp cooking functions: use it to quickly air fry, roast, bake, broil and dehydrate.

The Smart Programs make it fun and easy for anyone — from novice to chef — to prepare great healthy meals fast. And the bright displays, easy-to-use controls and easy-to-read icons that indicate cooking status make selecting programs and making adjustments simple — even during cooking. Customize the time and temperature selects for total control and save your presets so your favorite meals can be made the way you like them. And the Delay Start function ensures dinner is ready when you want it to be, and not before.

COOKING WITH INSTANT POT AIR FRYER CRISP

One appliance, two lids, infinite possibilities
Now you have every cooking method available at your fingertips. The pressure cooker lid offers 6 wet cooking functions: use it to quickly pressure cook, sauté, steam, slow cook, sous vide and warm. The Air Fryer lid offers 5 crisp cooking functions: use it to quickly air fry, roast, bake, broil and dehydrate.

Quick, healthy, amazing
Pressure cooking and air frying both help you save time and cook healthy meals, while roasting and baking with the air fryer lid produces amazing results — without using a lot of energy or heating up your kitchen.

Guilt-free frying in your Instant Pot
Get deep-fried taste and texture with little to no oil. EvenCrisp technology ensures tender juicy meals with a crisp, golden finish — every time. Now you can make perfect chicken wings, crispy french fries and onion rings, battered fried vegetables and more the healthy way.

Designed for convenience and ease
Wet and dry cooking function buttons are grouped together on the control panel. Pick your cooking technique with the touch of a button. Clean up is easy too. Sleek surfaces wipe clean. And the pot, air fry basket, and broil/dehydrating tray are all dishwasher safe.

FAQ: INSTANT POT AIR FRYER CRISP & FOOD

HOW MANY APPLIANCES DOES THE DUO CRISP+ AIR FRYER REPLACE?

The Instant Pot Duo Crisp + Air Fryer is capable of replacing your traditional pressure cooker, slow cooker, steamer, sauté pan, and food warmer. It also stands in as an air fryer, roaster, mini-oven, broiler and food dehydrator.

WHY DO I NEED TO DO THE INITIAL TEST RUN?

The Initial Test Run helps you become familiar with how your Instant Pot works, ensures the cooker is operating at peak performance, and sterilizes the cooking chamber so you can start preparing your delicious dishes right away.

CAN I USE THIRD PARTY ACCESSORIES WITH MY INSTANT POT?

To ensure the highest level of safety, we recommend only purchasing spare parts and accessories authorized by Instant Brands Inc.

HOW MUCH FOOD AND LIQUID SHOULD BE IN THE INNER POT WHEN COOKING?

For pressure cooking, if you aren't following a trusted recipe, pay attention to minimum liquid requirements and maximum fill lines as indicated on the inner pot.

For non-pressure cooking, the minimum liquid requirement listed below does not apply.

When using an air frying Smart Program, there should be little or no liquid in the inner pot. Avoid crowding the inner pot and cooking accessories when using these programs, as air needs to circulate freely to ensure proper cooking. Do not overfill the air fryer basket—food must not touch the heating element, or the element cover on the underside of the air fryer lid.

Minimum
The recommended minimum amount of liquid for pressure cooking, unless otherwise specified in a recipe, depends on the size of the cooker. If a recipe specifies a certain amount, always follow the recipe.

6 Quart: 1 ½ cups (12 oz / 375 mL)
Note: These liquids should be water-based, including stock, broth, juice, cooking sauces, as well as wine and beer. Oils and oil-based sauces do not have enough water content to account for the required liquid volume. Add suitable liquid to thin condensed cream-based soups and thick sauces.

Maximum
When pressure cooking, do not fill the inner pot higher than the PC MAX — 2/3 line as indicated on the inner pot.

When cooking foods that expand (e.g., rice, beans, pasta) do not fill the inner pot higher than the — 1/2 line as indicated on the inner pot.

Overfilling the inner pot may risk clogging the steam release and developing excess pressure. This may cause leakage, personal injuries, or damage to the cooker.

ARE THE PARTS FROM DIFFERENT MODELS OF INSTANT POT INTERCHANGEABLE?

Not always. It's a good idea to only use the parts that came with your Instant Pot, or authorized replacement parts and accessories that are designated for your size and model of Instant Pot.

In particular...

Using a pressure cooking lid from another model may result in improper sealing/locking, and is unsafe.
The air fryer lid is not compatible with other models of Instant Pot.
Instant Pot silicone sealing rings can be used in any matching size of Instant Pot pressure cooking lid.
Instant Pot inner pots can be used in any matching sized Instant Pot, except for the Duo Evo™ Plus, which features a new inner pot design.
If you need assistance choosing accessories or replacement parts, chat with one of our Customer Care agents.

WHAT IS THE INNER POT MADE OF?

The stainless steel inner pot is made primarily from 304 (18/8) stainless steel and is dishwasher safe.

The 3-ply bottom has an aluminum core for optimal heat dispersal, but no aluminum comes into contact with your food. With no chemical coating, the inner pot is compliant with FDA food safety standards.

The steam rack is also made from food grade 304 (18/8) stainless steel, so you can be sure that all of your food is cooked safely.

The air fryer basket has a ceramic non-stick coating, so food is easy to remove and the basket is easy to clean.

CAN I ADJUST MY SETTINGS AFTER COOKING HAS STARTED?

Yes! You can adjust the time, temperature and pressure level even after the Instant Pot has started cooking.

HOW DO I KNOW IF THE PRESSURE COOKING PROCESS HAS STARTED?

The Duo Crisp begins when you press Start, and displays On to indicate that pre-heating has begun. When the cooker builds up enough pressure the float valve rises, then the cooker beeps and counts down the cooking time.

HOW DO I KNOW WHEN IT'S SAFE TO OPEN THE LID AFTER PRESSURE COOKING?

Before opening the lid, make sure the float valve has dropped.

Do not attempt to open the lid if the float valve is still up.
Do not attempt to open the lid if it is locked and cannot be easily opened.
Do not force the lid open at any time.
If the float valve has not dropped, ensure the quick release button is pressed down into the Vent position. If no steam releases, use a long utensil to nudge the float valve down.

Note: When opening the lid, the inner pot may adhere to the lid. This is caused by vacuum due to cooling. To release the vacuum, press the quick release button down into the Vent position.

ARE THERE ANY FOODS I CAN'T PUT INTO THE INSTANT POT?

Ingredients that are high in sugar content may trigger the burn warning.

We recommend caution when cooking food such as applesauce, cranberries, pearl barley, oatmeal or other cereals, split peas, noodles, macaroni, rhubarb or spaghetti, as they tend to foam, froth or spatter and can cause clogging. When preparing these foods, do not fill the inner pot higher than the — 1/2 line as indicated on the inner pot and followed a trusted recipe.

Note: Regular cleaning of the lid and its parts (e.g., steam release handle, anti-block shield, steam release pipe and float valve) is important for proper function and to ensure the cooker's longevity.

BREAKFAST AND BRUNCH

BACON AND CROISSANT

COOKING TIME: 10 minutes | SERVES: 2

INGREDIENTS
- Thick-cut bacon – 4 pieces
- Croissants – 2, sliced
- Eggs – 2
- Butter – 1 tbsp.

For the sauce
- Ketchup – ½ cup
- Apple cider vinegar – 2 tbsps.
- Brown sugar – 1 tbsp.
- Molasses – 1 tbsp.
- Worcestershire sauce – ½ tbsp.
- Onion powder – ¼ tsp.
- Mustard powder – ¼ tsp.
- Liquid smoke – ¼ tsp.

DIRECTIONS
Preheat the air fryer to 390F. Mix all the sauce ingredients in a saucepan and heat until sauce thickens slightly. Place the bacon cuts flat on a tray and brush them with sauce on one side. Transfer to the air fryer basket with the brushed side up. Cook for 5 minutes then flip. Brush the other side with sauce and cook for 5 minutes more. Melt the butter in a pan and fry the eggs. Then place the eggs at the bottom of each croissant. Top them with two bacon slices each and close the croissant top. Serve.

AIR-FRIED FRENCH TOAST STICKS

COOKING TIME: 12 minutes | SERVES: 2

INGREDIENTS

- Sandwich bread – 4 pieces
- Softened butter – 2 tbsps.
- Eggs – 2, beaten
- Ground cloves – 1 pinch
- Cinnamon – 1 pinch
- Nutmeg – 1 pinch
- Salt – 1 pinch
- Maple syrup for garnish

DIRECTIONS

Preheat the air fryer to 350F. Beat the cinnamon, eggs, nutmeg, cloves, and salt in a bowl. Butter both sides of the bread slices and cut them into strips. Dredge each bread strip in the egg mixture. Arrange them in the air fryer basket. Cook for 2 minutes, then spray with cooking spray and flip. Cook the other side for 4 minutes. Careful not to burn. Drizzle with maple syrup and serve.

RANCHERO WRAPS

COOKING TIME: 8 minutes | SERVES: 2

INGREDIENTS

- Egg scramble – 2 Serves
- Flour tortillas – 2-large
- Corn tortillas – 2-small
- Pinto beans – 1/3 cup, cooked
- Ranchero sauce – ½ cup
- Avocado – ½, peeled and sliced
- Fresh jalapenos – 2, stemmed and sliced

DIRECTIONS

Assemble the large tortillas on a work surface. Arrange the crunch wraps by stacking the following ingredients in order: egg scramble, jalapeno, ranchero sauce, corn tortillas, avocado, and pinto beans. Fold to seal completely. Place one crunch wrap in the air fryer basket and cook at 350F for 6 minutes. Repeat and serve.

GARLIC BREAD

COOKING TIME: 5 minutes | SERVES: 4

INGREDIENTS
- Ciabatta – 4 slices
- Parmesan – ¼ cup, grated
- Salted butter – 1 tbsp.
- Garlic – 3 cloves, crushed
- Dried parsley to taste

DIRECTIONS
Preheat the air fryer to 360F. Melt the butter in a microwave. Add the garlic, cheese, and dried parsley to the bowl of butter. Spread the garlic mixture to both sides of ciabatta slices. Cook for 5 minutes. Serve.

SHRIMP AND RICE BREAKFAST FRITTATA

COOKING TIME: 15 minutes | SERVES: 4

INGREDIENTS
- Eggs – 4
- Pinch salt
- Dried basil – ½ tsp.
- Cooked rice – ½ cup
- Chopped cooked shrimp – ½ cup
- Baby spinach – ½ cup
- Grated cheese – ½ cup

DIRECTIONS
Beat the eggs with salt and basil until frothy in a bowl. Spray a pan with nonstick cooking spray. Combine the spinach, shrimp, and rice in the prepared pan. Pour the eggs in and sprinkle with the cheese. Bake at 320F until frittata is puffed and golden brown, about 14 to 18 minutes. Serve.

OMELETTE IN BREAD CUPS

COOKING TIME: 11 minutes | **SERVES:** 4

INGREDIENTS
- Crusty rolls – 4 (3-by-4-inch)
- Gouda – 4 thin slices
- Eggs – 5
- Heavy cream – 2 tbsps.
- Dried thyme – ½ tsp.
- Precooked bacon – 3 strips, chopped
- Salt and ground pepper to taste

DIRECTIONS
1. Cut the tops off the rolls and remove the insides to make a shell with about ½-inch of bread remaining. Use a slice of cheese to line the rolls, pressing down gently, so the cheese conforms to the inside of the roll. Beat the eggs and heavy cream in a bowl. Stir in the bacon, thyme, salt, and pepper. Pour the egg mixture into the rolls over the cheese. Bake at 330F until the eggs are puffy and starting to brown on top, about 8 to 12 minutes.

MIXED BERRY MUFFINS

COOKING TIME: 15 minutes | SERVES: 8

INGREDIENTS

- Flour – 1 1/3 cups, plus 1 tbsp.
- Baking powder – 2 tsps.
- White sugar – ¼ cup
- Brown sugar – 2 tbsps.
- Eggs – 2
- Whole milk – 2/3 cup
- Safflower oil – 1/3 cup
- Mixed fresh berries – 1 cup

DIRECTIONS

1. Combine the 1 1/3 cups flour, brown sugar, white sugar, and baking powder in a bowl and mix well. Combine the milk, eggs, and oil in another bowl and beat until mixed. Stir the egg mix into the dry ingredients. Mix until just combined. In another bowl, toss the mixed berries with the remaining 1 tbsp. flour until coated. Stir gently into the batter. Fold 16 foil muffin cups to make 8 cups. Put 4 cups into the basket and fill ¾ full with the batter. Bake at 320F until cooked, about 12 to 17 minutes. Repeat with the remaining batter and muffin cups. Cool and serve.

DUTCH PANCAKE

COOKING TIME: 15 minutes | SERVES: 4

INGREDIENTS

- Unsalted butter – 2 tbsps.
- Eggs – 3
- Flour – ½ cup
- Milk – ½ cup
- Vanilla – ½ tsp.
- Sliced fresh strawberries – 1 ½ cups
- Powdered sugar – 2 tbsps.

DIRECTIONS

Preheat the air fryer with a pan in the basket at 330F. Add the butter and melt. Meanwhile, beat the eggs, milk, flour, and vanilla in a bowl until frothy. Remove from the air fryer. Pour in the batter and tilt, so the butter covers the bottom of the pan and put back in the fryer. Bake at 330F until the pancake is puffed and golden brown, about 12 to 16 minutes. Remove and top with strawberries and powdered sugar. Serve.

SPINACH AND CHEESE OMELETTE

COOKING TIME: 8 minutes | SERVES: 2

INGREDIENTS

- Eggs – 3
- Shredded cheese – ½ cup
- Chopped fresh spinach – 2 tbsps.
- Salt and pepper to taste

DIRECTIONS

Whisk the eggs and with salt and pepper and place in a flat dish. Add the cheese and spinach. Do not stir. Cook at 390F for 8 minutes in the air fryer. Check the consistency of the omelette. Cook for another 2 minutes if a browner omelette is desired. Enjoy.

BAKED EGGS

COOKING TIME: 20 minutes | SERVES: 4

INGREDIENTS

- Eggs – 4
- Baby spinach – 1 pound, torn
- Ham – 7 ounces, chopped
- Milk – 4 tbsps.
- Olive oil – 1 tbsp.
- Cooking spray
- Salt and black pepper to taste

DIRECTIONS

Heat oil in a pan over medium heat. Add baby spinach and stir-fry for 2 minutes and remove from heat. Use cooking spray to grease 4 ramekins and divide ham and baby spinach in each. Crack an egg in each ramekin. Also divide milk, and season with salt and pepper. Place ramekins in the preheated air fryer at 350F and bake for 20 minutes. Serve.

BREAKFAST SOUFFLÉ

COOKING TIME: 8 minutes | SERVES: 4

INGREDIENTS

- Eggs – 4, whisked
- Heavy cream – 4 tbsps.
- Red chili pepper – 1 pinch crushed
- Parsley – 2 tbsps. chopped
- Chives – 2 tbsps. chopped
- Salt and black pepper to taste

DIRECTIONS

In a bowl, mix eggs with chives, parsley, red chili pepper, heavy cream, salt, and pepper. Mix well and divide into 4 soufflé dishes. Arrange dishes in the air fryer and cook at 350F for 8 minutes. Serve hot.

CINNAMON TOAST

COOKING TIME: 5 minutes | SERVES: 6

INGREDIENTS
- Butter – 1 stick, soft
- Bread – 12 slices
- Sugar – ½ cup
- Vanilla extract – 1 ½ tsps.
- Cinnamon powder – 1 ½ tsps.

DIRECTIONS
In a bowl, mix soft butter with cinnamon, vanilla, and sugar, and whisk well. Spread this on bread slices. Place them in the air fryer and cook at 400F for 5 minutes. Serve.

TURKEY BURRITO

COOKING TIME: 10 minutes | SERVES: 2

INGREDIENTS
- Turkey breast – 4 slices, cooked
- Red bell pepper – 1/2, sliced
- Eggs – 2
- Small avocado – 1, peeled, pitted, and sliced
- Salsa – 2 tbsps.
- Salt and black pepper to taste
- Mozzarella cheese – 1/8 cup, grated
- Tortillas for serving

DIRECTIONS
In a bowl, whisk the eggs with salt and pepper. Pour them in a pan and place in the air fryer's basket. Cook at 400F for 5 minutes. Remove and transfer eggs to a plate. Arrange tortillas on a working surface. Divide eggs, turkey meat, bell pepper, cheese, salsa, and avocado on them. Roll the burritos. Line the air fryer basket with tin foil and place the burritos on it. Heat up the burritos at 300F for 3 minutes. Serve.

VEGETABLES RECIPES

CAULIFLOWER BITES

COOKING TIME: 18 minutes | SERVES: 4

INGREDIENTS

- 1 Head Cauliflower, cut into small florets
- Tsps Garlic Powder
- Pinch of Salt and Pepper
- 1 Tbsp Butter, melted
- 1/2 Cup Chili Sauce
- Olive Oil

DIRECTIONS

1. 1 Preparing the Ingredients. Place cauliflower into a bowl and pour oil over florets to lightly cover.
2. Season florets with salt, pepper and the garlic powder and toss well.
3. 2 Air Frying. Place florets into the Instant Crisp Air Fryer, lock the air fryer lid and set at 350 degrees for 14 minutes.
4. Remove cauliflower from the Instant Crisp Air Fryer.
5. Combine the melted butter with the chili sauce
6. Pour over the florets so that they are well coated.
7. Return to the Instant Crisp Air Fryer and cook for additional 3 to 4 minutes
8. Serve as a side or with ranch or cheese dip as a snack

BUTTERED CARROT-ZUCCHINI WITH MAYO

COOKING TIME: 25 minutes | SERVES: 4

INGREDIENTS

- 1 tablespoon grated onion
- 2 tablespoons butter, melted
- 1/2-pound carrots, sliced
- 1-1/2 zucchinis, sliced
- 1/4 cup water
- 1/4 cup mayonnaise
- 1/4 teaspoon prepared horseradish
- 1/4 teaspoon salt
- 1/4 teaspoon ground black pepper
- 1/4 cup Italian bread crumbs

DIRECTIONS

1. 1 Preparing the Ingredients. Lightly grease baking pan of Instant Crisp Air Fryer with cooking spray. Add carrots. For 8 minutes, cook on 360°F. Add zucchini and continue cooking for another 5 minutes.
2. Meanwhile, in a bowl whisk well pepper, salt, horseradish, onion, mayonnaise, and water. Pour into pan of veggies. Toss well to coat.
3. In a small bowl mix melted butter and bread crumbs. Sprinkle over veggies.
4. 2 Air Frying. Lock the air fryer lid. Cook for 10 minutes at 390°F, until tops are lightly browned.
5. Serve and enjoy.

SAGE-BUTTER SPAGHETTI SQUASH

COOKING TIME: 12 minutes | SERVES: 6

INGREDIENTS

- One 3- to 3½-pound spaghetti squash, halved lengthwise and seeded
- 6 tablespoons unsalted butter
- 2 tablespoons packed fresh sage leaves, minced
- ½ teaspoon salt
- ½ teaspoon ground black pepper
- ½ cup finely grated Parmesan cheese (about 1 ounce)

DIRECTIONS

1. Preparing the Ingredients. Put the squash cut side up in the cooker; add 1 cup water.
2. High pressure for 12 minutes. Lock the lid on the Instant Crisp Air Fryer and then cook for 12 minutes. To get 12-minutes Cooking Time, press "Pressure" button, and use the Time Adjustment button to adjust the Cooking Time to 12 minutes.
3. Pressure Release. Use the quick-release method to bring the pot's pressure back to normal.
4. Finish the dish. Unlock and open the cooker. Transfer the squash halves to a cutting board; cool for 10 minutes. Discard the liquid in the cooker. Use a fork to scrape the spaghetti-like flesh off the skin and onto the cutting board; discard the skins.
5. Melt the butter in the electric cooker turned to its browning function. Stir in the sage, salt, and pepper, then add all of the squash. Stir and toss over the heat until well combined and heated through about 2 minutes. Add the cheese, toss well.
6. Close the Air Fryer Lid. Select BROIL, and set the time to 5 minutes. Select START to begin. Cook until top is browned.
7. Serve.

CHEDDAR, SQUASH, AND ZUCCHINI CASSEROLE

COOKING TIME: 30 minutes | SERVES: 4

INGREDIENTS

- 1 egg
- 5 saltine crackers, or as needed, crushed
- 2 tablespoons bread crumbs
- 1/2-pound yellow squash, sliced
- 1/2-pound zucchini, sliced
- 1/2 cup shredded Cheddar cheese
- 1-1/2 teaspoons white sugar
- 1/2 teaspoon salt
- 1/4 onion, diced
- 1/4 cup biscuit baking mix
- 1/4 cup butter

DIRECTIONS

1. 1 Preparing the Ingredients. Lightly grease baking pan of Instant Crisp Air Fryer with cooking spray. Add onion, zucchini, and yellow squash. Cover pan with foil and for 15 minutes, cook on 360° F or until tender.
2. Stir in salt, sugar, egg, butter, baking mix, and cheddar cheese. Mix well. Fold in crushed crackers. Top with bread crumbs.
3. 2 Air Frying Lock the air fryer lid. Cook for 15 minutes at 390° F until tops are lightly browned.
4. Serve and enjoy.

ZUCCHINI PARMESAN CHIPS

COOKING TIME: 8 minutes | SERVES: 10

INGREDIENTS

- ½ tsp. paprika
- ½ C. grated parmesan cheese
- ½ C. Italian breadcrumbs
- 1 lightly beaten egg
- 2 thinly sliced zucchinis

DIRECTIONS

1. 1 Preparing the Ingredients. Use a very sharp knife or mandolin slicer to slice zucchini as thinly as you can. Pat off extra moisture.
2. Beat egg with a pinch of pepper and salt and a bit of water.
3. Combine paprika, cheese, and breadcrumbs in a bowl.
4. Dip slices of zucchini into the egg mixture and then into breadcrumb mixture. Press gently to coat.
5. 2 Air Frying. With olive oil cooking spray, mist coated zucchini slices. Place into your Instant Crisp Air Fryer in a single layer. Lock the air fryer lid. Set temperature to 350°F, and set time to 8 minutes.
6. Sprinkle with salt and serve with salsa.

JALAPEÑO CHEESE BALLS

COOKING TIME: 8 minutes | SERVES: 12

INGREDIENTS

- 4 ounces cream cheese
- ⅓ cup shredded mozzarella cheese
- ⅓ cup shredded Cheddar cheese
- 2 jalapeños, finely chopped
- ½ cup bread crumbs
- 2 eggs
- ½ cup all-purpose flour
- Salt
- Pepper
- Cooking oil

DIRECTIONS

1. 1 Preparing the Ingredients. In a medium bowl, combine the cream cheese, mozzarella, Cheddar, and jalapeños. Mix well.
2. Form the cheese mixture into balls about an inch thick. Using a small ice cream scoop works well.
3. Arrange the cheese balls on a sheet pan and place in the freezer for 15 minutes. This will help the cheese balls maintain their shape while frying.
4. Spray the Instant Crisp Air Fryer basket with cooking oil. Place the bread crumbs in a small bowl. In another small bowl, beat the eggs. In a third small bowl, combine the flour with salt and pepper to taste, and mix well. Remove the cheese balls from the freezer. Dip the cheese balls in the flour, then the eggs, and then the bread crumbs.
5. 2 Air Frying. Place the cheese balls in the Instant Crisp Air Fryer. Spray with cooking oil. Lock the air fryer lid. Cook for 8 minutes.
6. Open the Instant Crisp Air Fryer and flip the cheese balls. I recommend flipping them instead of shaking so the balls maintain their form. Cook an additional 4 minutes. Cool before serving.

CRISPY ROASTED BROCCOLI

COOKING TIME: 8 minutes | SERVES: 2

INGREDIENTS

- ¼ tsp. Masala
- ½ tsp. red chili powder
- ½ tsp. salt
- ¼ tsp. turmeric powder
- 1 tbsp. chickpea flour
- 2 tbsp. yogurt
- 1 pound broccoli

DIRECTIONS

1. 1 Preparing the Ingredients. Cut broccoli up into florets. Soak in a bowl of water with 2 teaspoons of salt for at least half an hour to remove impurities.
2. Take out broccoli florets from water and let drain. Wipe down thoroughly.
3. Mix all other ingredients together to create a marinade.
4. Toss broccoli florets in the marinade. Cover and chill 15-30 minutes.
5. 2 Air Frying. Preheat the Instant Crisp Air Fryer to 390 degrees. Place marinated broccoli florets into the fryer, lock the air fryer lid, set temperature to 350°F, and set time to 10 minutes. Florets will be crispy when done.

CREAMY AND CHEESE BROCCOLI BAKE

COOKING TIME: 30 minutes | SERVES: 2

INGREDIENTS

- 1-pound fresh broccoli, coarsely chopped
- 2 tablespoons all-purpose flour
- salt to taste
- 1 tablespoon dry bread crumbs, or to taste
- 1/2 large onion, coarsely chopped
- 1/2 (14 ounce) can evaporated milk, divided
- 1/2 cup cubed sharp Cheddar cheese
- 1-1/2 teaspoons butter, or to taste
- 1/4 cup water

DIRECTIONS

1. 1 Preparing the Ingredients. Lightly grease baking pan of Instant Crisp Air Fryer with cooking spray. Mix in half of the milk and flour in pan and for 5 minutes, cook on 360°F. Halfway through cooking time, mix well. Add broccoli and remaining milk. Mix well and cook for another 5 minutes.
2. Stir in cheese and mix well until melted.
3. In a small bowl mix well, butter and bread crumbs. Sprinkle on top of broccoli.
4. 2 Air Frying. Lock the air fryer lid. Cook for 20 minutes at 360°F until tops are lightly browned.
5. Serve and enjoy.

COCONUT BATTERED CAULIFLOWER BITES

COOKING TIME: 20 minutes | SERVES: 4

INGREDIENTS

- salt and pepper to taste
- 1 flax egg (1 tablespoon flaxseed meal + 3 tablespoon water)
- 1 small cauliflower, cut into florets
- 1 teaspoon mixed spice
- ½ teaspoon mustard powder
- 2 tablespoons maple syrup
- 1 clove of garlic, minced
- 2 tablespoons soy sauce
- 1/3 cup oats flour
- 1/3 cup plain flour
- 1/3 cup desiccated coconut

DIRECTIONS

1. 1 Preparing the Ingredients..
2. In a mixing bowl, mix together oats, flour, and desiccated coconut. Season with salt and pepper to taste. Set aside.
3. In another bowl, place the flax egg and add a pinch of salt to taste. Set aside.
4. Season the cauliflower with mixed spice and mustard powder.
5. Dredge the florets in the flax egg first then in the flour mixture.
6. 2 Air Frying. Place inside the Instant Crisp Air Fryer, lock the air fryer lid and cook at 400°F or 15 minutes.
7. Meanwhile, place the maple syrup, garlic, and soy sauce in a sauce pan and heat over medium flame. Bring to a boil and adjust the heat to low until the sauce thickens.
8. After 15 minutes, take out the florets from the Instant Crisp Air Fryer and place them in the saucepan.
9. Toss to coat the florets and place inside the Instant Crisp Air Fryer and cook for another 5 minutes.

CRISPY JALAPENO COINS

COOKING TIME: 5 minutes | SERVES: 2

INGREDIENTS

- 1 egg
- 2-3 tbsp. coconut flour
- 1 sliced and seeded jalapeno
- Pinch of garlic powder
- Pinch of onion powder
- Pinch of Cajun seasoning (optional)
- Pinch of pepper and salt

DIRECTIONS

1. 1 Preparing the Ingredients. Ensure your Instant Crisp Air Fryer is preheated to 400 degrees.
2. Mix together all dry ingredients.
3. Pat jalapeno slices dry. Dip coins into egg wash and then into dry mixture. Toss to thoroughly coat.
4. Add coated jalapeno slices to Instant Crisp Air Fryer in a singular layer. Spray with olive oil.
5. 2 Air Frying. Lock the air fryer lid. Set temperature to 350°F, and set time to 5 minutes. Cook just till crispy.

BUFFALO CAULIFLOWER

COOKING TIME: 15 minutes | SERVES: 2

INGREDIENTS

- Cauliflower:
- 1 C. panko breadcrumbs
- 1 tsp. salt
- 4 C. cauliflower florets
- Buffalo Coating:
- ¼ C. Vegan Buffalo sauce
- ¼ C. melted vegan butter

DIRECTIONS

1. 1 Preparing the Ingredients. Melt butter in microwave and whisk in buffalo sauce.
2. Dip each cauliflower floret into buffalo mixture, ensuring it gets coated well. Hold over a bowl till floret is done dripping.
3. Mix breadcrumbs with salt.
4. 2 Air Frying. Dredge dipped florets into breadcrumbs and place into Instant Crisp Air Fryer. Lock the air fryer lid. Set temperature to 350°F, and set time to 15 minutes. When slightly browned, they are ready to eat!
5. Serve with your favorite keto dipping sauce!

CRISPED BAKED CHEESE STUFFED CHILE PEPPER

COOKING TIME: 30 minutes | SERVES: 3

INGREDIENTS

- 1 (7 ounce) can whole green Chile peppers, drained
- 1 egg, beaten
- 1 tablespoon all-purpose flour
- 1/2 (5 ounce) can evaporated milk
- 1/2 (8 ounce) can tomato sauce
- 1/4-pound Monterey Jack cheese, shredded
- 1/4-pound Longhorn or Cheddar cheese, shredded
- 1/4 cup milk

DIRECTIONS

1. 1 Preparing the Ingredients. Lightly grease baking pan of Instant Crisp Air Fryer with cooking spray. Evenly spread chilies and sprinkle cheddar and Jack cheese on top.
2. In a bowl whisk well flour, milk, and eggs. Pour over chilies.
3. 2 Air Frying. Lock the air fryer lid. For 20 minutes, cook on 360°F
4. Add tomato sauce on top.
5. Cook for 10 minutes at 390°F until tops are lightly browned.
6. Serve and enjoy.

JICAMA FRIES

COOKING TIME: 5 minutes | SERVES: 8

INGREDIENTS

- 1 tbsp. dried thyme
- ¾ C. arrowroot flour
- ½ large Jicama
- eggs

DIRECTIONS

1. 1 Preparing the Ingredients. Sliced jicama into fries.
2. Whisk eggs together and pour over fries. Toss to coat.
3. Mix a pinch of salt, thyme, and arrowroot flour together. Toss egg-coated jicama into dry mixture, tossing to coat well.
4. 2 Air Frying. Spray the Instant Crisp Air Fryer basket with olive oil and add fries. Lock the air fryer lid. Set temperature to 350°F, and set time to 5 minutes. Toss halfway into the cooking process.

JUMBO STUFFED MUSHROOMS

COOKING TIME: 20 minutes | SERVES: 4

INGREDIENTS

- 4 jumbo portobello mushrooms
- 1 tablespoon olive oil
- ¼ cup ricotta cheese
- 5 tablespoons Parmesan cheese, divided
- 1 cup frozen chopped spinach, thawed and drained
- ⅓ cup bread crumbs
- ¼ teaspoon minced fresh rosemary

DIRECTIONS

1. 1 Preparing the Ingredients. Wipe the mushrooms with a damp cloth. Remove the stems and discard. Using a spoon, gently scrape out most of the gills.
2. Rub the mushrooms with the olive oil.
3. 2 Air Frying Put in the Instant Crisp Air Fryer basket, hollow side up, lock the air fryer lid and bake for 3 minutes. Carefully remove the mushroom caps, because they will contain liquid. Drain the liquid out of the caps.
4. In a medium bowl, combine the ricotta, 3 tablespoons of Parmesan cheese, spinach, bread crumbs, and rosemary, and mix well.
5. Stuff this mixture into the drained mushroom caps. Sprinkle with the remaining 2 tablespoons of Parmesan cheese.
6. Put the mushroom caps back into the basket and bake for 4 to 6 minutes or until the filling is hot and the mushroom caps are tender.

AIR FRYER BRUSSELS SPROUTS

COOKING TIME: 10 minutes | SERVES: 8

INGREDIENTS
- ¼ tsp. salt
- 1 tbsp. balsamic vinegar
- 1 tbsp. olive oil
- 2 C. Brussels sprouts

DIRECTIONS
1. 1 Preparing the Ingredients. Cut Brussels sprouts in half lengthwise. Toss with salt, vinegar, and olive oil till coated thoroughly.
2. 2 Air Frying. Add coated sprouts to the Instant Crisp Air Fryer, close air fryer lid, set temperature to 400°F, and set time to 10 minutes. Shake after 5 minutes of cooking.
3. Brussels sprouts are ready to devour when brown and crisp!

SPAGHETTI SQUASH TOTS

COOKING TIME: 15 minutes | SERVES: 8

INGREDIENTS
- ¼ tsp. pepper
- ½ tsp. salt
- 1 thinly sliced scallion
- 1 spaghetti squash

DIRECTIONS
1. 1 Preparing the Ingredients. Wash and cut the squash in half lengthwise. Scrape out the seeds.
2. With a fork, remove spaghetti meat by strands and throw out skins.
3. In a clean towel, toss in squash and wring out as much moisture as possible. Place in a bowl and with a knife slice through meat a few times to cut up smaller.
4. Add pepper, salt, and scallions to squash and mix well.
5. 2 Air Frying. Create "tot" shapes with your hands and place in the Instant Crisp Air Fryer. Spray with olive oil. Lock the air fryer lid. Set temperature to 350°F, and set time to 15 minutes. Cook until golden and crispy!

CRISPY AND HEALTHY AVOCADO FINGERS

COOKING TIME: 10 minutes | SERVES: 4

INGREDIENTS

- ½ cup panko breadcrumbs
- ½ teaspoon salt
- 1 pitted Haas avocado, peeled and sliced
- liquid from 1 can white beans or aquafaba

DIRECTIONS

1. 1 Preparing the Ingredients. Preheat the Instant Crisp Air Fryer at 350°F.
2. In a shallow bowl, toss the breadcrumbs and salt until well combined.
3. Dredge the avocado slices first with the aquafaba then in the breadcrumb mixture.
4. Place the avocado slices in a single layer inside the Instant Crisp Air Fryer basket.
5. 2 Air Frying. Lock the air fryer lid. Cook for 10 minutes and shake halfway through the cooking time.

ONION RINGS

COOKING TIME: 10 minutes | SERVES: 4

INGREDIENTS

- 1 large spanish onion
- 1/2 cup buttermilk
- 2 eggs, lightly beaten
- 3/4 cups unbleached all-purpose flour
- 3/4 cups panko bread crumbs
- 1/2 teaspoon baking powder
- 1/2 teaspoon Cayenne pepper, to taste

DIRECTIONS

1. 1 Preparing the Ingredients. Start by cutting your onion into 1/2 thick rings and separate. Smaller pieces can be discarded or saved for other recipes.
2. Beat the eggs in a large bowl and mix in the buttermilk, then set it aside.
3. In another bowl combine flour, pepper, bread crumbs, and baking powder.
4. Use a large spoon to dip a whole ring in the buttermilk, then pull it through the flour mix on both sides to completely coat the ring.
5. 2 Air Frying. Lock the air fryer lid. Cook about 8 rings at a time in your Instant Crisp Air Fryer for 8-10 minutes at 360 degrees shaking half way through.

CINNAMON BUTTERNUT SQUASH FRIES

COOKING TIME: 10 minutes | **SERVES:** 8

INGREDIENTS
- 1 pinch of salt
- 1 tbsp. powdered unprocessed sugar
- ½ tsp. nutmeg
- 2 tsp. cinnamon
- 1 tbsp. coconut oil
- 10 ounces pre-cut butternut squash fries

DIRECTIONS
1. 1 Preparing the Ingredients. In a plastic bag, pour in all ingredients. Coat fries with other components till coated and sugar is dissolved.
2. 2 Air Frying. Spread coated fries into a single layer in the Instant Crisp Air Fryer. Lock the air fryer lid. Set temperature to 390°F, and set time to 10 minutes. Cook until crispy.

ROASTED ASPARAGUS

COOKING TIME: 10 minutes | **SERVES:** 4

INGREDIENTS
- Asparagus – 1 lb. ends trimmed
- Olive oil – 2 tsps.
- Salt and black pepper to taste

DIRECTIONS
Coat the asparagus with oil and season with salt and pepper. Cook in the air fryer at 380F for 7 to 10 minutes. Shake once. Serve.

CRISPY BROCCOLI

COOKING TIME: 10 minutes | SERVES: 4

INGREDIENTS

- Cooking oil – 2 tbsps.
- Broccoli – 1 lb. chopped
- Garlic powder – ½ tsp.
- Salt and pepper to taste
- Fresh lemon wedges

DIRECTIONS

Add broccoli to a bowl and drizzle with oil. Season with salt, pepper, and garlic powder. Mix and cook in the air fryer at 380F for 12 to 15 minutes. Shake the basket 3 times during cooking. Serve with lemon wedges.

ACORN SQUASH

COOKING TIME: 20 minutes | SERVES: 4

INGREDIENTS

- Acorn squash – 1, cut into half an inch thick cubes
- Butter – 3 tbsps. melted
- Brown sugar – 2 tsps.
- Kosher salt and black pepper to taste
- Chopped nuts and melted butter for topping

DIRECTIONS

1. In a bowl, combine melted butter, brown sugar, season with salt and pepper. Add in the acorn squash and mix. Cook in the air fryer at 375F for 15 to 20 minutes. Flip after 10 minutes of cooking. Serve with toppings.

FISH AND SEAFOOD

AIR FRYER SALMON

COOKING TIME: 15 minutes | SERVES: 2

INGREDIENTS
- Salmon fillets – 2 (6 ounces) fillets
- Olive oil – 2 tsps.
- Ground black pepper – ½ tsp.
- Mustard – 2 tbsps.
- Garlic – 1 clove, chopped
- Brown sugar -1 tbsp.
- Thyme leaves – ½ tsp.

DIRECTIONS
Rub the salmon with salt and pepper. Combine thyme, mustard, garlic, brown sugar, and oil in a bowl. Rub this mix on the salmon. Cook the salmon in the air fryer at 400F for 10 minutes. Flip at the halfway mark. Serve.

FISH FINGER SANDWICH

COOKING TIME: 15 minutes | SERVES: 4

INGREDIENTS

- Cod fillet – 13 ounces, skin removed
- Flour – 2 tbsps.
- Breadcrumbs -1 ½ ounces
- Capers – 12
- Frozen peas – 10 ounces
- Greek yogurt -1 tbsp.
- Lemon juice – 1 tbsp.
- Bread – 8 small slices
- Salt and pepper to taste
- Cooking oil spray

DIRECTIONS

Preheat the air fryer to 390F. Rub the fillet with salt and pepper. Place flour and breadcrumbs in separate bowls. Then coat the fillets in flour and in breadcrumbs. Spray with cooking oil and place in the air fryer. Cook at 390F for 15 minutes. Flip once at the halfway mark. Meanwhile. Boil the peas for 5 minutes or until tender. Then drain and put them in a blender. Add capers, yogurt, and lemon juice. Mix. Arrange the sandwich with bread, fish and pea puree. Serve.

TUNA PATTIES

COOKING TIME: 6 minutes | SERVES: 4

INGREDIENTS

- Canned tuna – 7 ounces
- Egg – 1
- Breadcrumbs – ¼ cup
- Mustard – 1 tbsp.
- Salt and pepper to taste
- Cooking spray

DIRECTIONS

Combine egg, tuna, bread crumbs, salt, pepper and mustard in a bowl. Make four patties with this mixture. Grease the air fryer basket with cooking oil. Cook the patties in Broil setting for 6 minutes. Flip the patties after 3 minutes. Serve.

GRILLED COD WITH SAUCE

COOKING TIME: 10 minutes | SERVES: 2

INGREDIENTS

- Cod fillets – 1 pound
- Olive oil – 2 tbsps.
- Lemon juice – 1 tbsp.
- Salt and pepper to taste

Sauce
- Heavy cream – ½ cup
- Ground mustard – 3 tbsps.
- Butter – 1 tbsp.
- Salt to taste

DIRECTIONS

Spread some oil on the fillets. Rub salt, pepper, and lemon juice on the fillets. Grease the air fryer basket and cook the fillets at 350F for 5 minutes. Then flip the fish and increase the temperature to 400F and cook for 5 minutes more. Meanwhile, add all the sauce ingredients in a saucepan and cook for 4 minutes or until thick. Serve cod with sauce.

RANCH AIR FRYER FISH FILLETS

COOKING TIME: 12 minutes | SERVES: 4

INGREDIENTS

- Tilapia fillets – 24 ounces
- Dry ranch-style dressing mix – 5 ounces
- Panko breadcrumbs – ¾ cup
- Eggs - 2
- Oil – 2 ½ tbsps.
- Lemon wedges- 4

DIRECTIONS

Mix the ranch dressing and breadcrumbs in a bowl. Add oil and mix again. Preheat the air fryer. Beat the eggs in a bowl. Dip the fillet in the egg mix then in the breadcrumbs. Coat well. Cook the fish in the air fryer at 360F for 12 minutes. Flip the fish at the halfway mark. Serve with lemon wedges.

TASTY COD

COOKING TIME: 12 minutes | SERVES: 4

INGREDIENTS

- Cod fillets – 2 (7-ounce) each
- Sesame oil – 1 drizzle
- Salt and black pepper to taste
- Water – 1 cup
- Dark soy sauce – 1 tsp.
- Light soy sauce – 4 tbsps.
- Sugar – 1 tbsp.
- Olive oil – 3 tbsps.
- Ginger – 4 slices
- Spring onions – 3, chopped
- Coriander – 2 tbsps. chopped

DIRECTIONS

Season fish with sesame oil, salt, and pepper. Rub well and leave aside for 10 minutes. Cook in the air-fryer at 356F for 12 minutes. Meanwhile, heat up a pot with water over medium heat. Add both soy sauces, and sugar, stir and bring to a simmer. Take off heat. Heat olive oil in a pan over medium heat. Add green onions, and ginger, stir, and cook for a few minutes and take off the heat. Divide fish on plates, top with green onions, and ginger. Drizzle with soy sauce mix, sprinkle coriander. Serve.

DELICIOUS CATFISH

COOKING TIME: 20 minutes | SERVES: 4

INGREDIENTS

- Catfish fillets – 4
- Salt and black pepper to taste
- A pinch of sweet paprika
- Parsley – 1 tbsp. chopped
- Lemon juice – 1 tbsp.
- Olive oil – 1 tbsp.

DIRECTIONS

Season catfish fillets with oil, paprika, pepper, and salt. Rub well. Cook in the air-fryer at 400F for 20 minutes. Flip the fish after 10 minutes. Divide fish on plates, drizzle lemon juice all over, sprinkle parsley and serve.

TABASCO SHRIMP

COOKING TIME: 10 minutes | SERVES: 4

INGREDIENTS

- Shrimp – 1 pound, peeled and deveined
- Red pepper flakes – 1 tsp.
- Olive oil – 2 tbsps.
- Tabasco sauce – 1 tsp.
- Water – 2 tbsps.
- Oregano – 1 tsp. dried
- Salt and black pepper to taste
- Dried parsley – ½ tsp.
- Smoked paprika – ½ tsp.

DIRECTIONS

In a bowl, mix water, oil, Tabasco sauce, shrimp, paprika, pepper, salt, parsley, oregano, and pepper flakes. Coat well. Transfer shrimp to preheated air fryer at 370F and cook for 10 minutes. Shake once. Serve.

BUTTERED SHRIMP SKEWERS

COOKING TIME: 6 minutes SERVES: 2

INGREDIENTS

- Shrimps – 8, peeled and deveined
- Garlic – 4 cloves, minced
- Salt and black pepper to taste
- Green bell pepper slices – 8
- Rosemary – 1 tbsp. chopped
- Butter – 1 tbsp. melted

DIRECTIONS

In a bowl, mix bell pepper slices, rosemary, pepper, salt, butter, garlic, and shrimp. Toss to coat and marinate for 10 minutes. Arrange 2 bell pepper slices and 2 shrimp on a skewer and repeat with the rest of the shrimp and bell pepper pieces. Cook them at 360F for 6 minutes. Serve.

ASIAN SALMON

COOKING TIME: 15 minutes | SERVES: 2

INGREDIENTS

- Salmon fillets – 2 medium
- Light soy sauce – 6 tbsps.
- Mirin – 3 tbsps.
- Water – 1 tsp.
- Honey – 6 tbsps.

DIRECTIONS

Mix soy sauce with water, honey, mirin and whisk well. Add salmon, rub well and marinate in the fridge for 1 hour. Cook at 360F for 15 minutes in the air-fryer. Flip once after 7 minutes. Meanwhile, put the soy marinade in a pan, and simmer and whisk on medium heat for 2 minutes. Divide salmon on plates. Drizzle marinade all over and serve.

AIR FRIED SALMON

COOKING TIME: 8 minutes SERVES: 2

INGREDIENTS
- Salmon fillets – 2
- Lemon juice – 2 tbsps.
- Salt and black pepper to taste
- Garlic powder – ½ tsp.
- Water – 1/3 cup
- Soy sauce – 1/3 cup
- Scallions – 3, chopped
- Brown sugar – 1/3 cup
- Olive oil – 2 tbsps.

DIRECTIONS
In a bowl, mix water, sugar, garlic powder, soy sauce, salt, pepper, oil, and lemon juice. Whisk well and add salmon fillets. Coat well and marinate in the refrigerator for 1 hour. Cook salmon in the air-fryer at 360F for 8 minutes. Flip once. Divide salmon on plates. Sprinkle scallions to the top and serve.

LEMONY SABA FISH

COOKING TIME: 8 minutes | SERVES: 2

INGREDIENTS
- Saba fish fillet – 4, boneless
- Salt and black pepper to taste
- Red chili pepper – 3, chopped
- Lemon juice – 2 tbsps.
- Olive oil – 2 tbsps.
- Garlic – 2 tbsps. minced

DIRECTIONS
Season fish fillets with salt and pepper and place in a bowl. Add garlic, chili, oil, and lemon juice and toss to coat. Transfer fish to the air fryer and cook at 360F for 8 minutes. Flipping halfway. Serve.

ASIAN HALIBUT

COOKING TIME: 10 minutes SERVES: 3

INGREDIENTS

- Halibut steaks – 1 pound
- Soy sauce – 2/3 cup
- Sugar – ¼ cup
- Lime juice – 2 tbsps.
- Mirin – ½ cup
- Red pepper flakes – ¼ tsp. crushed
- Orange juice – ¼ cup
- Ginger – ¼ tsp. grated
- Garlic – 1 clove, minced

DIRECTIONS

Pour soy sauce in a pan and heat over medium heat. Add garlic, ginger, pepper flakes, orange juice, lime, sugar, and mirin. Stir well, bring to a boil and take off the heat. Transfer half of the marinade to a bowl, add halibut, toss to coat and marinate in the refrigerator for 30 minutes. Cook halibut in the air fryer at 390F for 10 minutes. Flipping once. Divide halibut steaks on plates, drizzle the rest of the marinade all over and serve.

SHRIMP AND CRAB MIX

COOKING TIME: 25 minutes SERVES: 4

INGREDIENTS

- Yellow onion – ½ cup, chopped
- Green bell pepper – 1 cup, chopped
- Celery – 1 cup, chopped
- Shrimp – 1 cup, peeled and deveined
- Crabmeat – 1 cup, flaked
- Mayonnaise – 1 cup
- Worcestershire sauce – 1 tsp.
- Salt and black pepper to taste
- Breadcrumbs – 2 tbsps.
- Butter – 1 tbsp. melted
- Sweet paprika -1 tsp.

DIRECTIONS

In a bowl, mix crab meat, shrimp, onion, bell pepper, celery, mayo, salt, pepper and Worcestershire sauce. Transfer to a pan. Add melted butter, paprika, and bread crumbs. Coat well and place in the air fryer. Cook at 320F for 25 minutes. Shake once at the halfway mark. Serve.

SEAFOOD CASSEROLE

COOKING TIME: 40 minutes | SERVES: 6

INGREDIENTS

- Butter – 6 tbsps.
- Mushrooms – 2 ounces, chopped
- Green bell pepper – 1 small, chopped
- Celery – 1 stalk, chopped
- Garlic – 2 cloves, minced
- Small yellow onion – 1, chopped
- Salt and black pepper to taste
- Flour – 4 tbsps.
- White wine – ½ cup
- Milk – 1 ½ cups
- Heavy cream – ½ cup
- Sea scallops – 4, sliced
- Haddock – 4 ounces, skinless, boneless and cut into small pieces
- Lobster meat – 4 ounces, cooked and cut into small pieces
- Mustard powder – ½ tsp.
- Lemon juice – 1 tbsp.
- Bread crumbs – 1/3 cup
- Salt and black pepper to taste
- Cheddar cheese – 3 tbsps. grated
- Handful parsley, chopped
- Sweet paprika – 1 tsp.

DIRECTIONS

Heat 4 tbsps. of butter in a pan over a medium-high heat. Add wine, onion, garlic, celery, mushrooms, and bell pepper and cook for 10 minutes. Add milk, cream, and flour, stir well and cook for 6 minutes. Add haddock, lobster meat, scallops, mustard powder, salt, pepper, and lemon juice and stir well. Remove from heat and place in a pan. In a bowl, mix the rest of the butter with cheese, paprika, and bread crumbs and sprinkle over seafood mix. Transfer the pan to the air fryer and cook at 360F for 16 minutes. Serve garnish with parsley.

CRISPY CHEESY FISH FINGERS

COOKING TIME: 20 minutes | SERVES: 4

INGREDIENTS

- Large cod fish filet, approximately 6-8 ounces, fresh or frozen and thawed, cut into 1 ½-inch strips
- 2 raw eggs
- ½ cup of breadcrumbs (we like Panko, but any brand or home recipe will do)
- 2 tablespoons of shredded or powdered parmesan cheese
- 1 tablespoons of shredded cheddar cheese
- Pinch of salt and pepper

DIRECTIONS

1. 1 Preparing the Ingredients. Cover the basket of the Instant Crisp Air Fryer with a lining of tin foil, leaving the edges uncovered to allow air to circulate through the basket.
2. Preheat the Instant Crisp Air Fryer to 350 degrees.
3. In a large mixing bowl, beat the eggs until fluffy and until the yolks and whites are fully combined.
4. Dunk all the fish strips in the beaten eggs, fully submerging.
5. In a separate mixing bowl, combine the bread crumbs with the parmesan, cheddar, and salt and pepper, until evenly mixed.
6. One by one, coat the egg-covered fish strips in the mixed dry ingredients so that they're fully covered, and place on the foil-lined Instant Crisp Air Fryer basket.
7. 2 Air Frying. Close air fryer lid. Set the air-fryer timer to 20 minutes.
8. Halfway through the cooking time, shake the handle of the air-fryer so that the breaded fish jostles inside and fry-coverage is even.
9. After 20 minutes, when the fryer shuts off, the fish strips will be perfectly cooked and their breaded crust golden-brown and delicious! Using tongs, remove from the Instant Crisp Air Fryer and set on a serving dish to cool.

PANKO-CRUSTED TILAPIA

COOKING TIME: 10 minutes | SERVES: 3

INGREDIENTS
- 2 tsp. Italian seasoning
- 2 tsp. lemon pepper
- 1/3 C. panko breadcrumbs
- 1/3 C. egg whites
- 1/3 C. almond flour
- 3 tilapia fillets
- Olive oil

DIRECTIONS
1. Preparing the Ingredients. Place panko, egg whites, and flour into separate bowls. Mix lemon pepper and Italian seasoning in with breadcrumbs.
2. Pat tilapia fillets dry. Dredge in flour, then egg, then breadcrumb mixture.
3. Air Frying. Add to the Instant Crisp Air Fryer basket and spray lightly with olive oil. Close air fryer lid.
4. Cook 10-11 minutes at 400 degrees, making sure to flip halfway through cooking.

POTATO CRUSTED SALMON

COOKING TIME: 15 minutes | SERVES: 4

INGREDIENTS
- 1 pound salmon, swordfish or arctic char fillets, 3/4 inch thick
- 1 egg white
- 2 tablespoons water
- 1/3 cup dry instant mashed potatoes
- 2 teaspoons cornstarch
- 1 teaspoon paprika
- 1 teaspoon lemon pepper seasoning

DIRECTIONS
1. Preparing the Ingredients. Remove and skin from the fish and cut it into 4 serving pieces Mix together the egg white and water. Mix together all of the dry ingredients. Dip the filets into the egg white mixture then press into the potato mix to coat evenly.
2. Air Frying. Close air fryer lid in your Instant Crisp Air Fryer, cook at 360 degrees for 15 minutes, flip the filets halfway through.

SALMON CROQUETTES

COOKING TIME: 10 minutes | SERVES: 6-8

INGREDIENTS
- Panko breadcrumbs
- Almond flour
- 2 egg whites
- 2 tbsp. chopped chives
- 2 tbsp. minced garlic cloves
- ½ C. chopped onion
- 2/3 C. grated carrots
- 1 pound chopped salmon fillet

DIRECTIONS
1. Preparing the Ingredients. Mix together all ingredients minus breadcrumbs, flour, and egg whites.
2. Shape mixture into balls. Then coat them in flour, then egg, and then breadcrumbs. Drizzle with olive oil.
3. Air Frying. Add coated salmon balls to Instant Crisp Air Fryer, close air fryer lid and cook 6 minutes at 350 degrees. Shake and cook an additional 4 minutes until golden in color.

SNAPPER SCAMPI

COOKING TIME: 10 minutes | SERVES: 4

INGREDIENTS

- 4 (6-ounce) skinless snapper or arctic char fillets
- 1 tablespoon olive oil
- 3 tablespoons lemon juice, divided
- ½ teaspoon dried basil
- Pinch salt
- Freshly ground black pepper
- 2 tablespoons butter
- cloves garlic, minced

DIRECTIONS

1. 1 Preparing the Ingredients. Rub the fish fillets with olive oil and 1 tablespoon of the lemon juice. Sprinkle with the basil, salt, and pepper, and place in the Instant Crisp Air Fryer basket.
2. 2 Air Frying. Close air fryer lid and grill the fish for 7 to 8 minutes or until the fish just flakes when tested with a fork. Remove the fish from the basket and put on a serving plate. Cover to keep warm. In a 6-by-6-by-2-inch pan, combine the butter, remaining 2 tablespoons lemon juice, and garlic. Cook in the Instant Crisp Air Fryer for 1 to 2 minutes or until the garlic is sizzling. Pour this mixture over the fish and serve.

POULTRY RECIPES

THANKSGIVING TURKEY

COOKING TIME: 37 minutes | SERVES: 4

INGREDIENTS

- Turkey breast – 2 pounds
- Chopped thyme – 1 tsp.
- Chopped rosemary – 1 tsp.
- Maple syrup – ¼ cup
- Chopped sage – 1 tsp.
- Dijon mustard – 2 tbsps.
- Butter – 1 tbsp.
- Salt and pepper to taste
- Cooking spray

DIRECTIONS

Rub the turkey with salt and pepper. Rub thyme, rosemary, and sage on the turkey breasts. Combine butter, mustard, maple syrup in a bowl. Grease the air fryer basket with cooking spray. Cook the turkey in the air fryer for 35 minutes at 390F. Flip once at the halfway mark. Then remove the turkey and brush it with maple syrup sauce. Cook again for 2 minutes at 330F. Serve.

TURKEY BURGERS

COOKING TIME: 16 minutes | SERVES: 4

INGREDIENTS
- Turkey meat – 1 pound, ground
- Shallot – 1 minced
- A drizzle of olive oil
- Small jalapeno pepper – 1, minced
- Lime juice – 2 tsps.
- Zest from 1 lime, grated
- Salt and black pepper to taste
- Cumin – 1 tsp. ground
- Sweet paprika – 1 tsp.
- Guacamole for serving

DIRECTIONS
In a bowl, mix turkey meat with lime juice, zest, jalapeno, shallot, paprika, cumin, salt, and pepper. Mix well. Shape burgers from this mix and drizzle the oil over them. Cook in the preheated air fryer at 370F for 8 minutes on each side. Divide among plates and serve with guacamole on top.

HONEY DUCK BREASTS

COOKING TIME: 22 minutes | SERVES: 2

INGREDIENTS
- Smoked duck breast – 1, halved
- Honey – 1 tsp.
- Tomato paste – 1 tsp.
- Mustard – 1 tbsp.
- Apple vinegar – ½ tsp.

DIRECTIONS
Mix tomato paste, honey, mustard, and vinegar in a bowl. Whisk well. Add duck breast pieces and coat well. Cook in the air fryer at 370F for 15 minutes. Remove the duck breast from the air fryer and add to the honey mixture. Coat again. Cook again at 370F for 6 minutes. Serve.

CHINESE DUCK LEGS

COOKING TIME: 36 minutes | SERVES: 2

INGREDIENTS

- Duck legs – 2
- Dried chilies – 2, chopped
- Olive oil – 1 tbsp.
- Star anise – 2
- Spring onions – 1 bunch, chopped
- Ginger – 4 slices
- Oyster sauce – 1 tbsp.
- Soy sauce – 1 tbsp.
- Sesame oil – 1 tsp.
- Water – 14 ounces
- Rice wine – 1 tbsp.

DIRECTIONS

Heat oil in a pan. Add water, soy sauce, oyster sauce, ginger, rice wine, sesame oil, star anise, and chili. Stir and cook for 6 minutes. Add spring onions and duck legs, toss to coat and transfer to a pan. Place the pan in the air fryer and cook at 370F for 30 minutes. Serve.

DUCK BREASTS WITH ENDIVES

COOKING TIME: 25 minutes | SERVES: 4

INGREDIENTS

- Duck breasts – 2
- Salt and black pepper to taste
- Sugar – 1 tbsp.
- Olive oil – 1 tbsp.
- Endives – 6, julienned
- Cranberries – 2 tbsps.
- White wine – 8 ounces
- Garlic – 1 tbsp. minced
- Heavy cream – 2 tbsps.

DIRECTIONS

Score duck breasts and season with salt and pepper. Cook in the air fryer at 350F for 20 minutes. Flip once. Meanwhile, heat up a pan with oil over medium heat. Add endives, and sugar. Stir and cook for 2 minutes. Add salt, pepper, wine, garlic, cream, and cranberries — Stir-Fry for 3 minutes. Divide duck breasts on plates. Drizzle with the endives sauce and serve.

CREAMY COCONUT CHICKEN

COOKING TIME: 25 minutes | SERVES: 4

INGREDIENTS

- Big chicken legs – 4
- Turmeric powder – 5 tsps.
- Ginger – 2 tbsps. grated
- Salt and black pepper to taste
- Coconut cream – 4 tbsps.

DIRECTIONS

In a bowl, mix salt, pepper, ginger, turmeric, and cream. Whisk. Add chicken pieces, coat and marinate for 2 hours. Transfer chicken to the preheated air fryer and cook at 370F for 25 minutes. Serve.

CHINESE CHICKEN WINGS

COOKING TIME: 15 minutes | SERVES: 6

INGREDIENTS

- Chicken wings – 16
- Honey – 2 tbsps.
- Soy sauce – 2 tbsps.
- Salt and black pepper to taste
- White pepper – ¼ tsp.
- Lime juice – 3 tbsps.

DIRECTIONS

In a bowl, mix soy sauce, honey, salt, black pepper, lime juice, and white pepper. Whisk well. Add chicken pieces and coat well. Marinate in the refrigerator for 2 hours. Then cook in the air fryer at 370F for 6 minutes on each side. Then increase heat to 400F and cook for 3 minutes more. Serve.

HERBED CHICKEN

COOKING TIME: 40 minutes | SERVES: 4

INGREDIENTS

- Whole chicken – 1
- Salt and black pepper to taste
- Garlic powder – 1 tsp.
- Onion powder – 1 tsp.
- Thyme – ½ tsp. dried
- Rosemary – 1 tsp. dried
- Lemon juice – 1 tbsp.
- Olive oil – 2 tbsps.

DIRECTIONS

Season chicken with salt and pepper. Rub with onion powder, garlic powder, rosemary, and thyme. Rub with olive oil and lemon juice and marinate for 30 minutes. Cook chicken in the air fryer at 360F for 20 minutes on each side. Carve and serve.

CHICKEN PARMESAN

COOKING TIME: 15 minutes | SERVES: 4

INGREDIENTS

- Panko bread crumbs – 2 cups
- Parmesan – ¼ cup, grated
- Garlic powder – ½ tsp.
- White flour – 2 cups
- Egg – 1, whisked
- Chicken cutlets – 1 ½ pounds, skinless, and boneless
- Salt and pepper to taste
- Mozzarella - 1 cup, grated
- Tomato sauce – 2 cups
- Basil – 3 tbsps. chopped

DIRECTIONS

In a bowl, mix garlic powder, and parmesan and stir. Put flour in a second bowl and the egg in a third. Season chicken with salt, and pepper. Dip in flour, then in the egg mix and in panko. Cook chicken pieces in the air fryer at 360F for 3 minutes on each side. Transfer chicken to a baking dish. Add tomato sauce, and top with mozzarella. Cook in the air fryer at 375F for 7 minutes. Divide among plates, sprinkle basil on top and serve.

MEXICAN CHICKEN

COOKING TIME: 22 minutes | SERVES: 4

INGREDIENTS

- Salsa verde – 16 ounces
- Olive oil – 1 tbsp.
- Salt and black pepper to taste
- Chicken breast – 1 pound, boneless, and skinless
- Monetary Jack cheese – 1 ½ cups, grated
- Cilantro – ¼ cup, chopped
- Garlic powder – 1 tsp.

DIRECTIONS

Pour salsa verde in a baking dish. Season chicken with garlic powder, salt, pepper, and brush with olive oil. Place over the salsa verde. Place in the air fryer and cook at 380F for 20 minutes. Sprinkle cheese on top and cook 2 minutes more. Serve.

ITALIAN CHICKEN

COOKING TIME: 16 minutes | **SERVES:** 4

INGREDIENTS

- Chicken thighs – 8
- Olive oil – 1 tbsp.
- Garlic – 2 cloves, minced
- Thyme - 1 tbsp. chopped
- Heavy cream – ½ cup
- Chicken stock - ¾ cup
- Red pepper flakes – 1 tsp. crushed
- Parmesan – ¼ cup, grated
- Sun-dried tomatoes – ½ cup
- Basil – 2 tbsps. chopped
- Salt and black pepper to taste

DIRECTIONS

Season chicken with salt and pepper, and rub with half of the oil. Place in the preheated air fryer at 350F and cook for 4 minutes. Meanwhile, heat the rest of the oil in a pan and add garlic, thyme, pepper flakes, tomatoes, stock, heavy cream, salt, parmesan, and pepper. Bring to a simmer and remove from the heat. Place the mixture in a dish. Add chicken thighs on top and cook in the air fryer at 320F for 12 minutes. Serve with basil sprinkled on top.

CHICKEN SALAD

COOKING TIME: 10 minutes | SERVES: 4

INGREDIENTS

- Chicken breast – 1 pound, boneless, skinless and halved
- Cooking spray
- Salt and black pepper to taste
- Feta cheese – ½ cup, cubed
- Lemon juice – 2 tbsps.
- Mustard – 1 ½ tsps.
- Olive oil – 1 tbsp.
- Red wine vinegar – 1 ½ tsps.
- Anchovies – ½ tsp. minced
- Garlic – ¾ tsp. minced
- Water – 1 tbsp.
- Lettuce leaves – 8 cups, cut into strips
- Parmesan – 4 tbsps. grated

DIRECTIONS

Spray chicken breasts with cooking oil. Season with salt and pepper. Place in the air fryer and cook at 370F for 10 minutes. Flip once. Shred the chicken with 2 forks. Put in a salad bowl and mix with lettuce leaves. In the blender, mix feta cheese with lemon juice, olive oil, mustard, vinegar, garlic, anchovies, water and half of the parmesan and blend very well. Add this over the chicken mix. Toss and sprinkle the rest of the parmesan and serve.

BUFFALO CHICKEN TENDERS

COOKING TIME: 20 minutes | SERVES: 4

INGREDIENTS

- Boneless, skinless chicken tenders – 1 pound
- Hot sauce – ¼ cup
- Pork rinds – 1 ½ ounces, finely ground
- Chili powder – 1 tsp.
- Garlic powder – 1 tsp.

DIRECTIONS

Place chicken breasts in a bowl and pour hot sauce over them. Toss to coat. Mix ground pork rinds, chili powder and garlic powder in another bowl. Place each tender in the ground pork rinds, and coat well. With wet hands, press down the pork rinds into the chicken. Place the tender in a single layer into the air fryer basket. Cook at 375F for 20 minutes. Flip once. Serve.

TERIYAKI WINGS

COOKING TIME: 25 minutes | SERVES: 4

INGREDIENTS

- Chicken wings – 2 pounds
- Teriyaki sauce – ½ cup
- Minced garlic – 2 tsp.
- Ground ginger - ¼ tsp.
- Baking powder – 2 tsp.

DIRECTIONS

Except for the baking powder, place all ingredients in a bowl and marinate for 1 hour in the refrigerator. Place wings into the air fryer basket and sprinkle with baking powder. Gently rub into wings. Cook at 400F for 25 minutes. Shake the basket two or three times during cooking. Serve.

LEMONY DRUMSTICKS

COOKING TIME: 25 minutes | SERVES: 2

INGREDIENTS

- Baking powder – 2 tsps.
- Garlic powder – ½ tsp.
- Chicken drumsticks – 8
- Salted butter – 4 tbsps. melted
- Lemon pepper seasoning – 1 tbsp.

DIRECTIONS

Sprinkle garlic powder and baking powder over drumsticks and rub into chicken skin. Place drumsticks into the air fryer basket. Cook at 375F for 25 minutes. Flip the drumsticks once halfway through the cooking time. Remove when cooked. Mix seasoning and butter in a bowl. Add drumsticks to the bowl and toss to coat. Serve.

CRISPY SOUTHERN FRIED CHICKEN

COOKING TIME: 25 minutes | SERVES: 4

INGREDIENTS

- 1 tsp. cayenne pepper
- 2 tbsp. mustard powder
- 2 tbsp. oregano
- 2 tbsp. thyme
- 3 tbsp. coconut milk
- 1 beaten egg
- ¼ C. cauliflower
- ¼ C. gluten-free oats
- 8 chicken drumsticks

DIRECTIONS

1. 1 Preparing the Ingredients. Ensure the Instant Crisp Air Fryer is preheated to 350 degrees.
2. Lay out chicken and season with pepper and salt on all sides.
3. Add all other ingredients to a blender, blending till a smooth-like breadcrumb mixture is created. Place in a bowl and add a beaten egg to another bowl.
4. Dip chicken into breadcrumbs, then into egg, and breadcrumbs once more.
5. 2 Air Frying. Place coated drumsticks into the Instant Crisp Air Fryer. Lock the air fryer lid. Set temperature to 350°F, and set time to 20 minutes and cook 20 minutes. Bump up the temperature to 390 degrees and cook another 5 minutes till crispy.

CHICKEN ROAST WITH PINEAPPLE SALSA

COOKING TIME: 45 minutes | SERVES: 2

INGREDIENTS

- ¼ cup extra virgin olive oil
- ¼ cup freshly chopped cilantro
- 1 avocado, diced
- 1-pound boneless chicken breasts
- 2 cups canned pineapples
- 2 teaspoons honey
- Juice from 1 lime
- Salt and pepper to taste

DIRECTIONS

1. 1 Preparing the Ingredients. Preheat the Instant Crisp Air Fryer to 390°F.
2. Place the grill pan accessory in the Instant Crisp Air Fryer.
3. Season the chicken breasts with lime juice, olive oil, honey, salt, and pepper.
4. 2 Air Frying. Place on the grill pan, lock the air fryer lid and cook for 45 minutes.
5. Flip the chicken every 10 minutes to grill all sides evenly.
6. Once the chicken is cooked, serve with pineapples, cilantro, and avocado.

BEEF, LAMB AND PORK

LAMB WITH VEGGIES

COOKING TIME: 30 minutes | SERVES: 4

INGREDIENTS
- Carrot – 1, chopped
- Onion – 1, sliced
- Olive oil – ½ tbsp.
- Bean sprouts – 3 ounces
- Lamb loin – 8 ounces, sliced

For the marinade
- Garlic – 1 clove, minced
- Apple – ½, grated
- Salt and black pepper to taste
- Small yellow onion – 1, grated
- Grated ginger – 1 tbsp.
- Soy sauce – 5 tbsps.
- Sugar – 1 tbsp.
- Orange juice – 2 tbsps.

DIRECTIONS
In a bowl, mix 1 grated onion with black pepper, sugar, orange juice, soy sauce, 1 tbsp. ginger, garlic, and apple. Whisk and add the lamb. Coat and marinate for 10 minutes. Heat olive oil in a pan over a medium-high heat. Add 1 sliced onion, bean sprouts, and carrot. Stir-Fry for 3 minutes. Add lamb and the marinade. Place the pan in the preheat air fryer and cook at 360F for 25 minutes. Serve.

CREAMY LAMB

COOKING TIME: 1 hour | SERVES: 8

INGREDIENTS

- Leg of lamb – 5 pounds
- Buttermilk – 2 cups
- Mustard – 2 tbsps.
- Butter – ½ cup
- Basil – 2 tbsps. chopped
- Tomato paste – 2 tbsps.
- Garlic – 2 cloves, minced
- Salt and black pepper to taste
- White wine – 1 cup
- Cornstarch – 1 tbsp. mixed with 1 tbsp. water
- Sour cream – ½ cup

DIRECTIONS

Place lamb roast in a dish. Add buttermilk and toss to coat. Cover and marinate in the refrigerator for 24 hours. Pat dry lamb and put in a pan that fits in the air fryer basket. In a bowl, mix butter with garlic, salt, pepper, rosemary, basil, mustard, and tomato paste. Whisk well and spread over the lamb. Place in the air fryer and cook at 300F for 1 hour. Slice lamb, divide among plates. Heat up cooking juices from the pan on the stove. Add sour cream, salt, pepper, wine, and cornstarch mix. Remove from heat and drizzle lamb with this sauce. Serve.

LAMB SHANKS

COOKING TIME: 45 minutes | **SERVES:** 4

INGREDIENTS

- Lamb shanks – 4
- Yellow onion – 1, chopped
- Olive oil – 1 tbsp.
- Coriander seeds – 4 tsps. crushed
- White flour – 2 tbsps.
- Bay leaves – 4
- Honey – 2 tsps.
- Dry sherry – 5 ounces
- Chicken stock – 2 ½ cups
- Salt and pepper to taste

DIRECTIONS

Season the lamb shanks with salt and pepper. Rub with half of the oil and cook in the air fryer at 360F for 10 minutes. Heat up a pan that fits in the air fryer with the rest of the oil over medium-high heat. Add onion and coriander. Stir and cook for 5 minutes. Add salt, pepper, bay leaves, honey, stock, sherry, and flour. Stir, bring to a simmer, and add the lamb. Mix well. Cook in the air fryer at 360F for 30 minutes. Serve.

LAMB WITH POTATOES

COOKING TIME: 45 minutes | SERVES: 6

INGREDIENTS

- Lamb roast – 4 pounds
- Rosemary – 1 spring
- Garlic – 3 cloves, minced
- Potatoes – 6, halved
- Lamb stock – ½ cup
- Bay leaves – 4
- Salt and pepper to taste

DIRECTIONS

Put potatoes in a dish. Add salt, pepper, rosemary spring, garlic, bay leaves, stock, and lamb. Mix and place in the air fryer. Cook at 360F for 45 minutes. Slice lamb, divide among plates, and serve with potatoes and cooking juices.

CLASSIC MINI MEATLOAF

COOKING TIME: 25 minutes | SERVES: 6

INGREDIENTS

- 80/20 ground beef – 1 pound
- Yellow onion – ¼, diced
- Green bell pepper – ½, diced
- Egg – 1
- Almond flour – 3 tbsps.
- Worcestershire sauce – 1 tbsp.
- Garlic powder – ½ tsp.
- Dried parsley – 1 tsp.
- Tomato paste – 2 tbsps.
- Water – ¼ cup
- Powdered brown sugar – 1 tbsp.

DIRECTIONS

In a bowl, combine almond flour, egg, pepper, onion, and ground beef. Pour in Worcestershire sauce and add the parsley and garlic powder to the bowl. Mix well. Divide the mixture into two and place into two loaf baking pans. In another bowl, mix the sugar, water, and tomato paste. Spoon half the mixture over each loaf. Place loaf pans into the air fryer basket, working in batches. Cook at 350F for 25 minutes. Serve warm.

CHORIZO AND BEEF BURGER

COOKING TIME: 15 minutes | SERVES: 4

INGREDIENTS

- 80/20 ground beef – ¾ pound
- Ground chorizo – ¼ pound
- Chopped onion – ¼ cup
- Pickled jalapenos – 5 slices, chopped
- Chili powder – 2 tsps.
- Minced garlic -1 tsp.
- Cumin – ¼ tsp.

DIRECTIONS

Mix all the ingredients in a bowl. Make four burger patties from the mixture. Place burger patties into the air fryer basket. Cook at 375F for 15 minutes. Flip once. Serve.

STUFFED PEPPERS

COOKING TIME: 30 minutes | SERVES: 4

INGREDIENTS

- 80/20 ground beef – 1 pound
- Chili powder – 1 tbsp.
- Cumin – 2 tsps.
- Garlic powder – 1 tsp.
- Salt – 1 tsp.
- Ground black pepper – ¼ tsp.
- Diced tomatoes and green chilies – 1 (10-ounce) can, drained
- Green bell peppers – 4, cut in half (seeds and membrane removed)
- Shredded Monterey jack cheese – 1 cup, divided

DIRECTIONS

Brown the ground beef in the Instant Pot for 7 to 10 minutes on Sauté. Then drain the fat. Add cumin, chili powder, salt, black pepper, and garlic powder. Add drained tomatoes and chilies. Cook for 3 to 5 minutes. Spoon the cooked mixture evenly into bell pepper halves and top with ¼-cup cheese. Place the stuffed peppers into the air fryer basket. Cook at 350F for 15 minutes. Serve.

ITALIAN STUFFED BELL PEPPERS

COOKING TIME: 25 minutes | SERVES: 4

INGREDIENTS

- Ground pork Italian sausage – 1 pound
- Garlic powder – ½ tsp.
- Dried parsley – ½ tsp.
- Diced Roma tomato – 1
- Chopped onion – ¼ cup
- Green bell pepper – 4
- Shredded mozzarella cheese – 1 cup, divided

DIRECTIONS

Brown the ground sausage on Sauté in the Instant Pot until no longer pink. Drain fat. Add the onion, tomato, parsley, and garlic powder. Cook for 3 to 5 minutes more. Slice peppers in half and remove the seeds and white membrane. Spoon the meat mixture evenly into pepper halves. Top with mozzarella and place pepper halves into the air fryer basket. Cook at 350F for 15 minutes. Serve.

BACON CASSEROLE

COOKING TIME: 20 minutes | SERVES: 4

INGREDIENTS

- 80/20 ground beef – 1 pound
- White onion – ¼, chopped
- Shredded cheddar cheese – 1 cup, divided
- Egg – 1
- Bacon – 4 slices, cooked and crumbled
- Pickle spears – 2, chopped

DIRECTIONS

Brown the ground beef in the Instant Pot on Sauté for 7 to 10 minutes. Drain the fat. Add the ground beef to a bowl. Add egg, ½-cup cheddar and onion to the bowl. Mix well and add crumbled bacon. Pour the mixture into a round baking dish and top with remaining cheddar. Place into the air fryer basket. Cook at 375F for 20 minutes. Serve topped with chopped pickles.

SPICY LAMB SIRLOIN STEAK

COOKING TIME: 15 minutes | SERVES: 4

INGREDIENTS
- Onion – ½, chopped
- Ginger – 4 cubes, chopped
- Garlic – 5 cloves, chopped
- Garam masala – 1 tsp.
- Fennel – 1 tsp. ground
- Cinnamon – 1 tsp. ground
- Cayenne powder – ½ tsp.
- Salt – 1 tsp.
- Lamb sirloin – 1-pound, boneless

DIRECTIONS
Add all the ingredients in a blender except for the lamb chops and blend until paste. Make strips over the lamb chops. Rub the paste on the chops and mix well. Marinate overnight. Grease the air fryer basket. Place the lamb steaks in the air fryer grease with cooking spray. Bake at 380F for 15 minutes. Flip the meat at the halfway mark. Serve.

HERB RACK OF LAMB

COOKING TIME: 20 minutes | SERVES: 2

INGREDIENTS
- Whole rack of lamb – 1 pound
- Rosemary – 2 tbsps. dried
- Thyme – 1 tbsp. dried
- Garlic – 2 tsps. minced
- Salt and pepper to taste
- Olive oil – 4 tbsps.

DIRECTIONS
In a bowl, mix everything except for the lamb. Rub the lamb with the herb mixture and coat well. Cook in the air fryer at 360F for 10 minutes. Flip once at the halfway mark. Serve.

PULLED PORK

COOKING TIME: 2 ½ hours | SERVES: 8

INGREDIENTS
- Chili powder – 2 tbsps.
- Garlic powder – 1 tsp.
- Onion powder – ½ tsp.
- Ground black pepper – ½ tsp.
- Cumin – ½ tsp.
- Pork shoulder – 1 (4-pound)

DIRECTIONS
In a bowl, mix cumin, pepper, onion powder, garlic powder, and chili powder. Rub the spice mixture over the pork shoulder, patting it into the skin. Place the pork shoulder into the air fryer basket. Cook at 350F for 150 minutes. Shred the meat with forks and serve.

BABY BACK RIBS

COOKING TIME: 25 minutes | SERVES: 4

INGREDIENTS
- Baby back ribs – 2 pounds
- Chili powder – 2 tsps.
- Paprika – 1 tsp.
- Onion powder – ½ tsp.
- Garlic powder – ½ tsp.
- Ground cayenne pepper – ¼ tsp.
- Barbecue sauce – ½ cup

DIRECTIONS
Except for the barbecue sauce, rub ribs with the rest of the ingredients. Place into the air fryer basket. Cook at 400F for 25 minutes. Flip once. Brush ribs with barbecue sauce and serve.

JUICY PORK CHOPS

COOKING TIME: 15 minutes | SERVES: 2

INGREDIENTS

- Chili powder – 1 tsp.
- Garlic powder – ½ tsp.
- Cumin – ½ tsp.
- Ground black pepper – ¼ tsp.
- Dried oregano – ¼ tsp.
- Boneless pork chops – 2 (4-ounce)
- Unsalted butter – 2 tbsps. divided

DIRECTIONS

Mix oregano, pepper, cumin, garlic powder, and chili powder in a bowl. Rub dry rub onto pork chops. Place pork chops into the air fryer basket. Cook at 400F for 15 minutes. Serve each chop topped with 1 tbsp. butter.

REVERSE SEARED RIBEYE

COOKING TIME: 45 minutes | SERVES: 2

INGREDIENTS

- Ribeye steak – 1 (8-ounce)
- Salt – ½ tsp.
- Ground peppercorn – ¼ tsp.
- Coconut oil – 1 tbsp.
- Salted butter – 1 tbsp. softened
- Garlic powder – ¼ tsp.
- Dried parsley – ½ tsp.
- Dried oregano – ¼ tsp.

DIRECTIONS

Rub steak with salt and ground peppercorn. Place into the air fryer basket. Cook at 250F for 45 minutes. Check for doneness and cook a few minutes more if necessary. Remove the steak. Heat coconut oil in the Instant Pot on Sauté. Sear the steak until crisp and browned. Remove from heat and allow to rest. Whip butter with oregano, parsley, and garlic powder in a bowl. Slice steak and serve with herb butter on top.

BEEF AND BROCCOLI STIR-FRY

COOKING TIME: 20 minutes | SERVES: 2

INGREDIENTS

- Sirloin steak – ½ pound, thinly sliced
- Liquid aminos – 2 tbsps.
- Grated ginger – ¼ tsp.
- Finely minced garlic – ¼ tsp.
- Coconut oil – 1 tbsp.
- Broccoli florets – 2 cups
- Crushed red pepper – ¼ tsp.
- Xanthan gum – 1/8 tsp.
- Sesame seeds – ½ tsp.

DIRECTIONS

In a bowl, add coconut oil, garlic, ginger, liquid aminos, and beef. Cover and marinate 1 hour in the refrigerator. Remove beef from the marinade, reserving marinade, and place the beef into the air fryer basket. Cook at 320F for 20 minutes. After 10 minutes, add broccoli and sprinkle red pepper into the air fryer basket and shake. Bring the marinade to a boil in a skillet, then reduce heat to simmer. Stir in xanthan gum and allow to thicken. When cooking is done, add the beef and broccoli from the air fryer to the skillet and toss. Sprinkle with sesame seeds and serve.

BBQ MEATBALLS

COOKING TIME: 14 minutes | SERVES: 4

INGREDIENTS

- 80/20 ground beef – 1 pound
- Ground Italian sausage – ¼ pound
- Egg – 1
- Onion powder – ¼ tsp.
- Garlic powder – ½ tsp.
- Dried parsley - 1 tsp.
- Bacon – 4 slices, cooked and chopped
- Chopped white onion – ¼ cup
- Chopped pickled jalapenos – ¼ cup
- Barbecue sauce – ½ cup

DIRECTIONS

Mix ground beef, sausage and egg in a bowl until fully combined. Mix in all remaining ingredients except barbecue sauce. Make 8 meatballs. Place meatballs into the air fryer basket. Cook at 400F for 14 minutes. Turn once. Remove meatballs from the fryer and toss in barbecue sauce. Serve.

PORK SALAD

COOKING TIME: 8 minutes | SERVES: 2

INGREDIENTS

- Coconut oil – 1 tbsp.
- Pork chops – 2 (4-ounce) chopped into 1-inch cubes
- Chili powder – 2 tsps.
- Paprika – 1 tsp.
- Garlic powder – ½ tsp.
- Onion powder – ¼ tsp.
- Chopped romaine – 4 cups
- Roma tomato – 1 medium, diced
- Shredded Monterey jack cheese – ½ cup
- Avocado – 1, diced
- Full-fat ranch dressing – ¼ cup
- Chopped cilantro – 1 tbsp.

DIRECTIONS

Drizzle coconut oil over the pork and sprinkle with onion powder, garlic powder, paprika, and chili powder. Place pork into the air fryer basket. Cook at 400F for 8 minutes. In a bowl, place crispy pork, tomato, and romaine. Top with shredded cheese and avocado. Pour ranch dressing around the bowl and toss to coat. Top with cilantro. Serve.

SNACKSAND APPETIZER

PROSCIUTTO-PARMESAN ASPARAGUS

COOKING TIME: 10 minutes | SERVES: 4

INGREDIENTS

- Asparagus – 1 pound
- Prosciutto – 12 (0.5 ounce) slices
- Coconut oil – 1 tbsp. melted
- Lemon juice – 2 tsps.
- Red pepper flakes – 1/8 tsp.
- Grated Parmesan cheese – 1/3 cup
- Salted butter – 2 tbsps. melted

DIRECTIONS

On a clean work surface, place a few asparagus spears onto a sliced of prosciutto. Drizzle with lemon juice and coconut oil. Sprinkle Parmesan and red pepper flakes across asparagus. Roll prosciutto around asparagus spears. Place into the air fryer basket. Repeat. Cook at 375F and 10 minutes. Drizzle the asparagus rolls with butter before serving.

BACON-WRAPPED JALAPENO POPPERS

COOKING TIME: 12 minutes | SERVES: 4

INGREDIENTS

- Jalapenos – 6, membrane and seeds removed (about 4" long each)
- Full-fat cream cheese – 3 ounces
- Shredded medium cheddar cheese – 1/3 cup
- Garlic powder – ¼ tsp.
- Bacon – 12 slices

DIRECTIONS

Place cream cheese, cheddar, and garlic powder in a bowl. Microwave for 30 seconds and stir. Spoon cheese mixture into hollow jalapenos. Wrap a slice of bacon around each jalapeno half, completely covering pepper. Place into the air fryer basket. Cook at 400F for 12 minutes. Flip once. Serve.

GARLIC PARMESAN CHICKEN WINGS

COOKING TIME: 25 minutes | SERVES: 4

INGREDIENTS

- Raw chicken wings – 2 pounds
- Salt – 1 tsp.
- Garlic powder – ½ tsp.
- Baking powder – 1 tbsp.
- Unsalted butter – 4 tbsps. melted
- Grated Parmesan cheese – 1/3 cup
- Dried parsley – ¼ tsp.

DIRECTIONS

Place chicken wings, salt, ½ tsp. garlic powder, and baking powder in a bowl. Coat and place wings into the air fryer basket. Cook at 400F for 25 minutes. Toss the basket two or 3 times during the cooking time. Combine butter, parmesan, and parsley in a bowl. Remove wings from the air fryer and place into a bowl. Pour the butter mixture over the wings and toss to coat. Serve warm.

BUFFALO CHICKEN DIP

COOKING TIME: 10 minutes | SERVES: 4

INGREDIENTS
- Cooked chicken breast – 1 cup, diced
- Full-fat cream cheese – 8 ounces, softened
- Buffalo sauce – ½ cup
- Full-fat ranch dressing – 1/3 cup
- Chopped pickled jalapenos – 1/3 cup
- Shred cheddar cheese – 1 ½ cups, divided
- Scallions – 2, sliced

DIRECTIONS
Place chicken into a large bowl. Add buffalo sauce, cream cheese, and ranch dressing. Stir to mix well. Fold in jalapenos and 1-cup cheddar. Pour the mixture into a round baking dish and place remaining cheddar on top. Place dish into the air fryer basket. Cook at 350F for 10 minutes. Top with sliced scallions and serve warm.

CHEESE BREAD

COOKING TIME: 15 minutes | SERVES: 4

INGREDIENTS
- Shredded mozzarella cheese – 2 cups
- Grated parmesan cheese – ¼ cup
- Chopped pickled jalapenos – ¼ cup
- Eggs – 2
- Bacon – 4 slices, cooked and chopped

DIRECTIONS
Mix all ingredients in a bowl. Cover the air fryer basket with parchment paper. Press out the mixture into a circle with damp hands. Or you can make two smaller circles. Place the cheese bread into the air fryer basket. Cook at 320F for 15 minutes. Flip the bread with 5 minutes remaining. The bread should be golden brown when fully cooked. Serve warm.

CHEESEBURGER DIP

COOKING TIME: 10 minutes | SERVES: 6

INGREDIENTS

- Full-fat cream cheese – 8 ounces
- Full-fat mayonnaise – ¼ cup
- Full-fat sour cream – ¼ cup
- Chopped onion – ¼ cup
- Garlic powder – 1 tsp.
- Worcestershire sauce -1 tbsp.
- Shredded cheddar cheese – 1 ¼ cups, divided
- Cooked 80/20 ground beef – ½ pound
- Bacon – 6 slices, cooked and crumbled
- Large pickle spears – 2, chopped

DIRECTIONS

Place cream cheese in a bowl, and microwave for 45 seconds. Stir in sour cream, mayonnaise, onion, garlic powder, 1-cup cheddar, and Worcestershire sauce. Add cooked bacon and ground beef. Sprinkle remaining cheddar on top. Place in a bowl and put into the air fryer basket. Cook at 400F for 10 minutes. The dip is done when the top is golden and bubbling. Sprinkle pickles over the dish. Serve warm.

PORK RIND TORTILLAS

COOKING TIME: 5 minutes | SERVES: 4

INGREDIENTS

- Pork rinds – 1 ounce, ground
- Shredded mozzarella cheese – ¾ cup
- Full-fat cream cheese – 2 tbsps. chopped
- Egg – 1

DIRECTIONS

Place mozzarella into a bowl. Add cream cheese then to the bowl. Microwave for 30 seconds, or until both types of cheese are melted. Add the egg and ground pork rinds to the cheese mixture. Stir and make a ball. Separate the dough into four small balls. Place each ball of dough between two sheets of parchment and roll into a ¼ flat layer. Place tortillas into the air fryer basket in a single layer. Set the temperature to 400F and cook for 5 minutes. Serve.

MOZZARELLA STICKS

COOKING TIME: 10 minutes | SERVES: 3

INGREDIENTS

- Mozzarella string cheese sticks – 6 (1-ounce)
- Grated Parmesan cheese – ½ cup
- Pork rinds – ½ ounce, finely ground
- Dried parsley – 1 tsp.
- Eggs – 2

DIRECTIONS

Cut the mozzarella sticks in half. Freeze until firm. In a bowl, mix ground pork rinds, Parmesan, and parsley. Whisk eggs in another bowl. Dip a frozen mozzarella stick into beaten eggs and then into the Parmesan mixture to coat. Repeat with the remaining sticks. Place mozzarella stick into the air fryer basket. Cook at 400F for 10 minutes or until golden. Serve warm.

BACON-WRAPPED ONION RINGS

COOKING TIME: 10 minutes | SERVES: 4

INGREDIENTS

- Large onion – 1, sliced into ¼ inch thick slices
- Sriracha – 1 tbsp.
- Bacon – 8 slices

DIRECTIONS

Brush sriracha over the onion slices. Take two slices of onion and wrap bacon around the rings. Repeat with the remaining onion and bacon. Place into the air fryer basket. Cook at 350F for 10 minutes. Flip the onion rings halfway through the cooking time. Serve warm.

SWEET PEPPER POPPERS

COOKING TIME: 8 minutes | SERVES: 4

INGREDIENTS

- Mini sweet peppers – 8 (seeds and membranes removed)
- Full-fat cream cheese – 4 ounces, softened
- Bacon – 4 slices, cooked and crumbled
- Shredded pepper jack cheese – ¼ cup

DIRECTIONS

In a bowl, mix bacon, cream cheese, and pepper jack. Place 3 tsps. of the mixture into each sweet pepper and press down firmly. Place in the air fryer basket. Cook at 400F for 8 minutes. Serve warm.

SPICY SPINACH ARTICHOKE DIP

COOKING TIME: 10 minutes | SERVES: 6

INGREDIENTS

- Frozen spinach – 10 ounces, drained and thawed
- Artichoke hearts – 1 (14-ounce) can, drained and chopped
- Chopped pickled jalapenos – ¼ cup
- Full-fat cream cheese – 8 ounces, softened
- Full-fat sour cream – ¼ cup
- Full-fat mayonnaise – ¼ cup
- Garlic powder – ½ tsp.
- Grated Parmesan cheese – ¼ cup
- Shredded pepper jack cheese – 1 cup

DIRECTIONS

Mix all ingredients in a baking bowl. Place into the air fryer basket. Cook at 320F for 10 minutes. Serve warm.

POTATO WEDGES

COOKING TIME: 25 minutes | SERVES: 4

INGREDIENTS

- Potatoes – 2, cut into wedges
- Olive oil – 1 tbsp.
- Salt and black pepper to taste
- Sour cream – 3 tbsps.
- Sweet chili sauce – 2 tbsps.

DIRECTIONS

In a bowl, mix potato wedges with oil, salt, and pepper. Toss well. Add to the air fryer basket and cook at 360F for 25 minutes. Flip once. Divide potato wedges onto plates. Drizzle chili sauce and sour cream all over and serve.

MUSHROOM DISH

COOKING TIME: 8 minutes | SERVES: 4

INGREDIENTS

- Button mushrooms – 10, stems removed
- Italian seasoning – 1 tbsp.
- Salt and black pepper to taste
- Cheddar cheese – 2 tbsps. grated
- Olive oil – 1 tbsp.
- Mozzarella – 2 tbsps. grated
- Dill – 1 tbsp. chopped

DIRECTIONS

In a bowl, mix mushrooms with oil, seasoning, dill, salt, and pepper. Mix well. Arrange mushrooms in your air fryer basket, sprinkle mozzarella and cheddar in each and cook them at 360F for 8 minutes. Divide them between plates and serve.

SWEET POTATO FRIES

COOKING TIME: 20 minutes | SERVES: 2

INGREDIENTS

- Sweet potatoes – 2, peeled and cut into medium fries
- Salt and black pepper to taste
- Olive oil – 2 tbsps.
- Curry powder – ½ tsp.
- Coriander – ¼ tsp. ground
- Ketchup – ¼ cup
- Mayonnaise – 2 tbsps.
- Cumin – ½ tsp. ground
- Ginger powder – 1 pinch
- Cinnamon powder – 1 pinch

DIRECTIONS

In the air fryer's basket, mix sweet potato fries with salt, pepper, coriander, curry powder, and oil. Toss well. Cook at 370F for 20 minutes. Flipping once. Meanwhile, in a bowl, mix ketchup with cinnamon, ginger, cumin, and mayo. Whisk well. Divide fries on plates. Drizzle ketchup mix over them and serve.

CORN WITH LIME AND CHEESE

COOKING TIME: 15 minutes | SERVES: 2

INGREDIENTS

- Corns on the cob – 2, husks removed
- A drizzle of olive oil
- Feta cheese – ½ cup, grated
- Sweet paprika – 2 tsps.
- Juice from 2 limes

DIRECTIONS

Rub corn with oil and paprika. Place in the air fryer basket and cook at 400F for 15 minutes. Flip once. Divide corn on plates, sprinkle cheese on top. Drizzle with lime juice and serve.

DESSERTS

MUG CAKE

COOKING TIME: 25 minutes | SERVES: 1

INGREDIENTS
- Egg – 1
- Coconut flour – 2 tbsps.
- Heavy whipping cream – 2 tbsps.
- Granular erythritol – 2 tbsps.
- Vanilla extract – ¼ tsp.
- Baking powder – ¼ tsp.

DIRECTIONS
Whisk egg in a 4-inch ramekin. Then add the remaining ingredients and mix. Stir until smooth. Place into the air fryer basket. Cook at 300F for 25 minutes. Serve.

POUND CAKE

COOKING TIME: 25 minutes | SERVES: 6

INGREDIENTS
- Almond flour – 1 cup
- Salted butter – ¼ cup, melted
- Granular erythritol – ½ cup
- Vanilla extract – 1 tsp.
- Baking powder – 1 tsp.
- Full-fat sour cream – ½ cup
- Full-fat cream cheese – 1 ounce, softened
- Eggs – 2

DIRECTIONS
Mix erythritol, butter, and flour in a bowl. Add in cream cheese, sour cream, baking powder, and vanilla. Mix well. Add eggs and mix. Pour batter into a 6-inch round baking pan. Place the pan into the air fryer basket. Cook at 300F for 25 minutes. Cool and serve.

CHOCOLATE MAYO CAKE

COOKING TIME: 25 minutes | SERVES: 6

INGREDIENTS
- Almond flour – 1 cup
- Salted butter – ¼ cup, melted
- Granular erythritol – ½ cup, plus 1 tbsp.
- Vanilla extract – 1 tsp.
- Full-fat mayonnaise – ¼ cup
- Unsweetened cocoa powder – ¼ cup
- Eggs – 2

DIRECTIONS
Mix all the ingredients in a bowl until smooth. Pour batter into a round baking pan. Place the pan into the air fryer basket. Cook at 300F for 25 minutes. Cool and serve.

RASPBERRY DANISH BITES

COOKING TIME: 7 minutes | SERVES: 10

INGREDIENTS

- Almond flour – 1 cup
- Baking powder – 1 tsp.
- Granular swerve – 3 tbsps.
- Full-fat cream cheese – 2 ounces, softened
- Egg – 1
- Raspberry preserve – 10 tsps.

DIRECTIONS

Mix all ingredients except preserve in a bowl and make a dough. Place the bowl in the freezer for 20 minutes, then roll it to make 10 balls. Press gently in the center of each ball. Place 1 tsp. preserves in the center of each ball. Line the air fryer basket with parchment. Place each Danish bite on the parchment. Press down gently to flatten the bottom. Cook at 400F for 7 minutes. Cool and serve.

PEANUT BUTTER COOKIES

COOKING TIME: 8 minutes | SERVES: 8

INGREDIENTS

- Smooth peanut butter – 1 cup
- Granular erythritol – 1/3 cup
- Egg – 1
- Vanilla extract – 1 tsp.

DIRECTIONS

Mix all the ingredients in a bowl until smooth. Continue to stir until the mixture begins to thicken. Roll the mixture into eight balls and press gently down to flatten into 2-inch round disks. Line the air fryer basket with parchment. Place the cookies onto the parchment. Work in batches if necessary. Cook at 320F for 8 minutes. Flip the cookies at the 6-minute mark. Serve.

CINNAMON CREAM PUFFS

COOKING TIME: 6 minutes | SERVES: 8

INGREDIENTS

- Almond flour – ½ cup
- Vanilla protein powder – ½ cup
- Granular erythritol – ½ cup
- Baking powder – ½ tsp.
- Egg – 1
- Unsalted butter – 5 tbsps. melted
- Full-fat cream cheese – 2 ounces
- Powdered erythritol – ¼ tsp.
- Ground cinnamon – ¼ tsp.
- Heavy whipping cream – 2 tbsps.
- Vanilla extract – ½ tsp.

DIRECTIONS

Mix butter, egg, baking powder, granular erythritol, protein powder, and flour in a bowl to make a dough. Keep the dough in the freezer for 20 minutes. Roll the dough with wet hands to make eight balls. Line the air fryer basket with parchment. Place the dough balls into the air fryer basket. Cook at 380F for 6 minutes. Flip halfway through the cooking time. Remove and cool the puffs. In a bowl, beat cream, cream cheese, powdered erythritol, cinnamon, and vanilla until fluffy. Cut a small hole in the bottom of each puff and fill with some of the cream mixtures. Serve.

MOLTEN LAVA CAKES

COOKING TIME: 12 minutes | SERVES: 4

INGREDIENTS

- Self-raising flour – 1.5 tbsps.
- Baker's sugar – 3.5 tbsps.
- Unsalted butter – 3.5 oz.
- Dark chocolate – 3.5 oz. chopped
- Eggs – 2

DIRECTIONS

Preheat the air fryer to 375F. Grease and flour 4 ramekins. Melt butter and dark chocolate in the microwave. Stirring throughout. Mix sugar and egg until frothy and pale. Pour melted chocolate mixture into the egg mixture. Stir in flour and mix everything. Fill the ramekins about ¾ full with batter. Bake in the air fryer at 375F for 10 minutes. Remove, cool and serve.

CHOCOLATE CAKE II

COOKING TIME: 30 minutes | SERVES: 6

INGREDIENTS

- Eggs – 3
- Sour cream – ½ cup
- Flour – 1 cup
- Sugar – 2/3 cup
- Butter – 1 stick, room temperature
- Cocoa powder – 1/3 cup
- Baking powder – 1 tsp.
- Baking soda – ½ tsp.
- Vanilla – 2 tsps.

DIRECTIONS

Preheat air fryer to 320F. Mix the wet ingredients in a bowl and dry ingredients in another. Gradually pour the dry mixture into the wet. Lightly mix. Place in the air fryer basket. Cook for 25 minutes. Check if the cake is done, if not then cook for another 5 more minutes. Cool on a wire rack.

CHEESECAKE BITES

COOKING TIME: 7 minutes | SERVES: 2

INGREDIENTS

- Cream cheese – 8 oz. softened
- Erythritol – ½ cup, plus 2 tbsps.
- Vanilla extract – ½ tsp.
- Almond flour – ½ cup
- Heavy cream – ½ packet

DIRECTIONS

Mix the cream cheese with ½ packet heavy cream, ½-cup erythritol, and vanilla extract until smooth. Scoop the mixture onto a parchment paper-lined baking sheet. Freeze for 30 minutes for the best results. Mix the almond flour with 2 tbsps. of erythritol in a bowl. Roll the frozen bites into the almond flour mixture. Place the cheesecake bites into the air fryer basket and cook for 7 minutes at 370F.

BROWNIES

COOKING TIME: 20 minutes | SERVES: 6

INGREDIENTS

- Almond flour – ½ cup
- Powdered erythritol – ½ cup
- Unsweetened cocoa powder – 2 tbsps.
- Baking powder – ½ tsp.
- Unsalted butter – ¼ cup, softened
- Egg – 1
- Chopped pecans – ¼ cup
- Chocolate chips – ¼ cup

DIRECTIONS

Mix almond flour, baking powder, cocoa powder, and erythritol in a bowl. Stir in egg and butter. Fold in chocolate chips and pecans. Scoop mixture into a baking pan and place the pan into the air fryer basket. Cook at 300F for 20 minutes. Cool, slice and serve.